SEXUAL
HEALING

SEXUAL HEALING

A Resource Book for a Healthy and Happy Sex Life

MARY O'CONOR

TOWN
HOUSE
DUBLIN

First published in 2002 by

TownHouse and CountryHouse Ltd
Trinity House
Charleston Road
Ranelagh
Dublin 6
Ireland

1 3 5 7 9 10 8 6 4 2

A CIP catalogue record for this book is available from the
British Library.

ISBN: 1-86059-153-1

Cover and Text Design by Anú Design
Illustrations by Michael Cole

Printed and bound by
Cox & Wyman Ltd, Reading, Berkshire.

CONTENTS

For the three most important men in my life
— John, Hugh and Keith, with love.

ACKNOWLEDGEMENTS

When I approached Treasa Coady of TownHouse with the idea of the book she was enthusiastic and continued to be supportive throughout the entire project. Marie Heaney and Claire Rourke subsequently helped guide me gently and with humour through the editing process. Jill Stevens was my very first tutor and I want to acknowledge how much I value her role in my development. Thank you to Caroline and Professor Robert Harrison and also Dr Edgar Mocanu at the Rotunda Hospital. Thanks to Dr Emer Keeling for her medical input, her constant good humour and for introducing me to golf – and to all my colleagues in the Albany Clinic in Dublin. A special thank you to my son Keith for his endless patience in teaching me everything I know about computers. I am very lucky to have as my best friend Carol O'Duffy, who is the sister I never had and has been a constant support to me throughout the years. A final and very special acknowledgement must go to my clients, who have shared their lives, bared their souls and trusted me to be of some help to them. It has been a privilege to work with you all.

INTRODUCTION

A few things that happened in quick succession led me to write this book. Firstly, I saw a husband and wife in the clinic who found it very difficult to tell me why they had come to see me. Eventually she plucked up the courage and told me that, although they had been married for nine years, they had never had intercourse. "There," she said, "I've finally said it. Nobody else in the world knows about this except you," and she watched me to gauge my reaction. She was totally taken aback when I told her that by no means did she beat the record in the cases I had seen. She had no idea that anybody else could have experienced what she had, that it was the condition that I see most frequently and that it was treatable. Secondly, one of my clients, who I had been seeing for some time, told me that it was her understanding that penetration could only be attempted after the woman had reached orgasm and she found this very difficult. Thirdly, a male client, an avid football player, with whom I was doing a basic information session, told me he felt incredibly stupid. "Up until this moment I did not realise I was circumcised. I'm an only child, nobody ever talked to me about sex and I always felt a freak in the shower with the other guys as I felt I had a piece missing from my penis."

So I got to thinking that there are lots of sex manuals out there – some great, some not so good – but none had a particularly Irish slant or addressed the sexual problems prevalent in Ireland, which are brought about by specific cultural and religious influences. In the chapters that follow, I want to share my thoughts with you about sex in general: perhaps to allay some fears, to give some information in a non-scientific way and, hopefully, to encourage you to explore your own sexuality and your view on sex so that you can have a happier, more fulfilling and enjoyable sex life.

Throughout the book, when I refer to clients, the names have been changed, as have any details that may make them recognisable.

Mary O'Conor
March 2002

[1]

SEXUAL
MYTHS

A man is ready, willing and able to have sex at all times

This is a view perpetrated by books, films and television. I mean when did you ever see erectile problems or premature ejaculation feature in a movie (apart from the teenager in *American Pie* [1999])? There is never any question that a man might be stressed from work, feeling bad about his body or any number of things that would interfere with his libido. I remember one man coming to see me. He had erectile difficulties and had been sent along by his wife to get himself fixed. We spoke for some time and I began to explore the state of the relationship between them. He then volunteered the information, "I cannot stand her – she is a bully and everything I do is wrong, including the way I make love." When I suggested that this state of affairs could be contributing to his erectile difficulties he found it hard to believe.

Apart from relationship problems or work stresses, there is a lot of what we call 'performance anxiety' for men. For instance, I have lost count of the number of very young men who have come to see me saying that they are really wary of the club scene because it is expected that, once they 'get off' with a girl, they are expected to have sex with her and, because of a previous bad experience, they are frightened that they will not be able to perform or that they will perform badly. They tend to avoid the situation altogether rather than be faced with what they would see as failure.

I remember a guy, whom I shall call Joe, coming to see me about his problems with premature ejaculation. He was a very handsome thirty-two-year-old with a warm personality and a successful career, but he had never gone on more than two dates with any woman. He knew that, if he did, it would inevitably lead to being fully sexual and then he would be 'found out'. I wondered out loud as to what the girls thought about all of this. Did they sometimes think, "Oh, I wasn't attractive/witty/clever enough for him to want to see me again"? This had never even crossed Joe's mind. All he was concerned about was that he was simply no good to women and the only way out was to avoid getting involved with them, even though he would have loved to be in a relationship and to share his life with somebody. However, anybody meeting Joe at work or going on a date with him would have absolutely no idea about all those insecurities going on inside his brain.

The man is responsible for the woman's orgasm

More pressure on the poor man! Let's get this straight – everybody is responsible for their *own* orgasm, but it seems normal for the woman to blame the guy when she doesn't have one. I never hear a man complaining that the woman didn't give him an ejaculation, but I often hear women say "he doesn't give me an orgasm". An orgasm is all about letting go and some people find it more difficult to let go than others, but that does not mean it is their partner's fault! I deal with lack of orgasm in another section but, in the meantime, please let go of this myth.

Sex equals intercourse

We are far too penetration oriented and, in the minds of an awful lot of people, sex equals intercourse. Sometimes people tell me that they have decided to wait until after they are married to have sex. This is something I do not have a problem with, what I *do* have a problem with is the fact that they were doing absolutely everything else except having sexual intercourse before they were married, so please don't tell me they were not having sex.

I remember counselling one couple who had an extremely stormy relationship. She had had an affair, but was adamant that she had not been unfaithful. She maintained that all they had was mutual oral sex but that wasn't *really* sex and she had not been unfaithful at all. Not surprisingly her husband had some problems with this concept. I feel people can be sexual in all sorts of ways. Sometimes people (early on in treatment with me) tell me that, when a ban is put on actual intercourse, they feel more free and relaxed in all sorts of ways and find themselves being much more sensual and much more tactile. In other words, when the threat of intercourse has been removed – and for whatever reason at that particular time they perceive intercourse as a threat – they can relax and be truly sexual.

What if somebody suffers from a physical disability whereby intercourse is not possible? They can still have a happy and fulfilling sex life – it just does not include intercourse. A group of women that I have found to be extremely sexual are those suffering with vaginismus, a condition that does not allow penetration to take place at all. However, they have worked out their own ways of being sexual and are highly orgasmic and usually enjoy a sexual life. Certainly sexual intercourse is the preferred way for conception – although nowadays, due to advances in fertility procedures, that is not always the case – but unless one is trying for a baby it is not necessary for a successful sexual encounter to include intercourse.

'Coming' together is the ultimate goal

For a start, 'coming' together or simultaneous orgasm, to use the technical term, is difficult, and there is a danger of getting tied up in performance anxiety to 'get it right' to the detriment of everything else. In all the years I have been working with couples I have only once encountered a couple who, as a matter of course, came together. They thought everybody did and were amazed to find they were in a minority. They were coming to see me because of his lack of desire and it did nothing to help his libido to know that, when they did have sex, they would climax at the same time. If you take an average lovemaking session as lasting thirty minutes, including foreplay and after-chat, and take an average orgasm/ejaculation as lasting ten to fifteen seconds it doesn't take a great mathematician to work out that the odds of the couple's fifteen seconds happening at the same time are pretty slim. Add to that the fact that 75 per cent of women achieve orgasm before or after intercourse and most men ejaculate during it and you have even less of a possibility of it happening simultaneously. And it really should not matter. What should matter is that having sex is a mutually enjoyable experience with no pressure on either partner. By the way, I'm not saying that coming together is not possible and not something to be aimed for, I'm just saying that it should not be the ultimate goal.

If you fantasise, you are being unfaithful

A lot of people get very fearful when the word fantasy is mentioned. They are afraid that they won't be able to fantasise or feel that if they do they are somehow being unfaithful to their partner. Indeed on one occasion a young couple came to me for counselling because she was unable to reach orgasm. I explained that part of the treatment would involve her using fantasy and he was so appalled at the prospect that he actually walked out of the session.

So what is fantasy? It is the ability to suspend reality and let the imagination run riot. By doing this you are enabling yourself to enter into another world, one where anything may happen and where you, yourself, may direct the action. Rather like writing your own film script really; one that can have many variations, many endings, one with yourself in the starring role – or maybe not taking part at all – but always with things happening as you would wish. We start using our imagination at a very early age when we are playing with our toys but, generally, it is in masturbation that our fantasies become sexual.

Some people have a very active imagination and their minds alone provide enough material for them. Others use books, films, videos, magazines and, more recently, the internet to assist in their arousal for masturbatory purposes. Some couples also use some of these things to help in their mutual arousal, particularly a video that they may watch together to help get them going, after which they turn off the video and carry on with the real thing. One client told me that the only problem with this was sore knees. However, sometimes women are unhappy with their men using material, which they consider demeaning to women, as masturbatory aids. This is fair enough and, if this *is* the case, the onus is on the man either to stop using the material or to make absolutely sure that the woman never has to confront it.

Much more subtle is the question of being unfaithful through fantasy. Some people are appalled that their partner may be fantasising about somebody else when making love and others feel guilty for doing it. But I have to ask, who are they harming? It is only fantasy after all. Of course it is a different story if somebody decides to move their fantasy into reality and instead of *imagining* what it is like to have great sex with, say, the gym instructor, they actually go ahead and have it while already in a committed relationship. It goes without saying that acting out fantasies can cause all sorts of problems, but as long as fantasies remain fantasies then I cannot see the problem.

The American writer Nancy Friday has written some very good books on fantasies. For women there is *My Secret Garden* (Hutchinson, London, 1979) and *Women On Top* (Hutchinson, London, 1991), while the male equivalent, *Men in Love* (Hutchinson, London, 1980), is well worth browsing through.

Sex abuse equals penetration of some form

All the recent revelations regarding sexual abuse of children has made us terribly aware of this horrible cancer in our society. The whole area of abuse is dealt with in Chapter 11, however, I feel that the myth exists that, unless penetration of some form took place, then there was really no abuse at all. I often find that the abused person will say things to me like, "Well it wasn't really all that bad when I read of other cases in the newspaper." Yet they are suffering serious psychological damage as a result of what happened to them and, in most cases, there are sexual or emotional problems, or both. I have learned over the years that I get far more information as regards sexual abuse from clients when I ask them if anybody ever touched them in any way that made them feel uncomfortable, rather than ask them if they were ever abused. Asking them if they were ever shown any pictures or told any stories of a sexual nature that were inappropriate can also elicit a positive response. Anything that is inappropriate can be termed abuse.

I remember Hanna coming to see me because she had vaginismus (and so could not allow penetration), and she and her husband were anxious to start a family. She had gone to her GP who advised her to purchase some vaginal dilators and work with them herself. This she had done diligently for over a year and was still not able to allow penetration. When I was taking down her history I asked her the 'inappropriate touching' question and she was able to tell me about her cousin who used to take her to a river bed near where she lived and have her sit on his lap and rub against his erect penis, which she could remember feeling even through the clothes. He would have her sitting with her back against his chest and even now that position in any sort of foreplay made her extremely tense. She was not inclined to view this as a form of abuse until I got her to visualise somebody doing the same thing to her niece whom she adored and who was the same age as she was when the episodes with her cousin happened. We did an amount of work around the abuse and she responded very successfully to treatment. (Their child was conceived shortly afterwards.)

Women receive more stimulation from a larger penis – size matters

A lot of men are very concerned about penis size, and a lot of women are not. Actually the most concern I hear from women is from those who have a problem with penetration and are concerned that their man's penis is too big, but when I talk to the partners themselves they assure me that they are just average – 'family size' as a friend of mine defines it. I firmly believe that size does *not* matter, bearing in mind, firstly, that the vagina has no nerve endings in it and therefore a woman has very little sensitivity inside the vagina. (For example a woman would find it very hard to tell if the man is using a condom unless she sees it.) Secondly, the vagina expands and lengthens to accept whatever goes into it – whether it is one or two fingers, a vibrator, a penis, or a baby's head on its way out. As Bernard Zilbergeld, who has written the wonderful *The New Male Sexuality* (Bantam, New York, 1999), points out "the vagina is a potential rather than a space". So whether the penis is slightly below or slightly above average it will all feel the same to the woman, her vagina is concerned with hugging whatever penis is in there, regardless of size. Isn't nature wonderful!

Sometimes men are very concerned that they are abnormally small. I try to reassure them by showing them photographs of lots penises of different shapes and sizes, circumcised and uncircumcised, and explain that, when they are looking down at themselves they are actually looking at a foreshortened penis and, therefore, not seeing what everybody else is seeing. If they are still unhappy, I send them to consult with one of the doctors in the clinic. Not one of them has come back to report that there is anything amiss.

Most women do not masturbate

Oh yes, they do! They just don't talk about it as much as men do. Women use masturbation for all the same reasons as men do. When they are feeling horny, when they want to get to sleep, when they become aroused through watching a movie or reading. They masturbate when they have no partner and when they have, although, as with men, if they are having a satisfactory sex life then they do not feel the need to masturbate, or at least not as often as if they had no partner. It is true that some women do not masturbate because they did not discover it earlier on in their lives, and some choose not to on religious grounds. Men find it a bit daunting that a woman can bring herself to climax in about two-and-a-half minutes whereas when he is with her, it may take about a half an hour!

The reasons for this is that a woman knows her own body so well, she knows exactly what works for her and she can also be totally uninhibited.

I remember working with Clara whose boyfriend was really anxious for her to masturbate while he was there as he had never seen her orgasm. Clara was loath to do this as she achieved climax by rocking her body in a foetal position and clenching and unclenching her vaginal muscles (no hands!). She was very embarrassed about this and couldn't contemplate doing it in front of Frank. However, we negotiated that she would do it in the dark and he promised to keep his eyes closed. This worked for them and she eventually graduated to doing it with the light on outside in the corridor.

Sex should be spontaneous

When I suggest to couples that they set aside time to do the exercises I give them, quite often there is an objection that it is very clinical to actually *plan* sessions and that they would much rather that they just happen. However, they are coming to me because things are *not* happening, or at least not to their satisfaction. So what is so wrong with planning? We plan all sorts of things and then look forward to them like mad. I know I love looking forward to my holidays and always like to know well in advance when the next one is going to be so that I can look forward to it. When a couple first meets they make dates and look forward to them. The same is true for lovemaking. It can be really nice to actually arrange to go to bed early, or whatever the couple's shorthand is for getting together, and then anticipate their time together. I am currently working with a gay couple who send each other e-mails to remind themselves that they had planned to be sexual that evening. Naturally they have developed their own particular way of saying it in case somebody else reads their mails, but they have fun with it.

Men who wear women's underwear are homosexual

Some men get a thrill from wearing women's underwear, particularly when they are in a sexual situation, but this most certainly does not make them homosexual. In my experience, the biggest problem that these men have is that, in many cases, their partners are not turned on – indeed they are quite turned off – by the thought of their man in female underwear. Often men will say that they are very sorry that they ever told their partners about their fetish because it has become a great bone of contention between them. The compromise that is usually reached is that underwear is used only for masturbation purposes. This means that nobody is forced to take part in any act with which they feel uncomfortable.

An exception to the usual was Jean who came to see me in quite a state, having discovered Visa bills to a mail order underwear store in her husband's bedside table. She immediately jumped to the conclusion that he was having an affair and was sending his new lady underwear. She was utterly devastated. She eventually tackled him about her discovery only to find out that the underwear was for himself. I think she was so relieved to find that there was not another woman in his life that she was able to accept what he was doing and subsequently allowed it occasionally in their sex life. I saw herself and Mark on a number of occasions and she gained a lot of insight into the whole area of sexuality in our times together. However, I have to say that, in my experience of similar situations, Jean's reaction would be the exception rather than the rule. This is a very delicate subject for couples and one that requires a lot of understanding from a partner.

Apart from the question of women's underwear, which would be viewed as a fetish, there is of course the whole area of cross-dressing, which again raises doubts in people's minds about sexual orientation. A man who likes to wear women's clothes, and is therefore termed a transvestite, can be either straight or gay. (There is no female equivalent.) So there are heterosexual males who cross-dress and usually find it sexually arousing. However, I have spoken to other men who maintain that they find it purely relaxing to cross-dress and insist that, for them, there is no sexual element in it at all.

Some cross-dressers will spend part of their time as a normal heterosexual male and part as a female. I remember having a cross-dresser on my radio programme who arrived for the interview in full female attire – wig, nail varnish, complete make-up, the lot – and who gave the listeners a very insightful view as to what it was like to be a cross-dresser. After the programme, he went into the gents and after only about five minutes reappeared as a very handsome man in pinstripe suit, shirt and tie. We went to the pub for a pint where he told me all about his wife and three children.

There are also homosexual transvestites who will cross-dress – often very flamboyantly à la Danny La Rue – but who will only be interested in attracting males.

Transsexuals are yet another sector wherein individuals believe themselves to be a woman or a man, respectively, trapped in the wrong body. They will dress according to their preferred gender with no particular sexual significance attached and will often seek medical help to change their bodies to be consistent with how they feel themselves to be. This is a very slow and painful process and one that should not be undertaken lightly and certainly not without a lot of specialised counselling.

[2]

THE AROUSAL
PROCESS IN
MEN

I am aware that, as a woman writing about men and their arousal process, I could be accused of not knowing what I am talking about. However, over the years so many men have shared their experiences, difficulties and thoughts with me that I feel I can represent them with some insight. I have to say that I think men get a bad press and I get mad when I see them depicted as being 'only after the one thing' and 'once they are satisfied they roll over and go to sleep'. The men that have come to consult with me, either alone or with their partners, have all been really concerned with their performance as lovers and their ability to satisfy their partners. This is true of all ages – I have seen men from nineteen to seventy-eight – and I think they are all wonderful to care enough to try to make things better.

As I wrote 'performance' it struck me that what is hugely different between men and women's role in the sexual act is that men have to *perform*. They have to get the erection, keep the erection and ejaculate. All these things require them to *do* things that cannot be faked. The woman, on the other hand, can use a lubricant if she is not lubricating naturally, can fake an orgasm (and if she is a good actress he need never know) and she does not need to have an orgasm in order to achieve a pregnancy.

Penis size

This is something that can cause a lot of worry for some men. Just like breasts, penises come in different sizes and widths and there is no 'right' size. I can truly say I have never heard a woman complain about her lover's penis being too small whereas I have often heard this fear expressed by men. I have heard women speak fearfully about a large penis, but this is very often related to a female dysfunction where, in her mind, the penis has taken on enormous proportions. The male in question will almost always tell me that he is just about average.

Men who think they have a very small penis say they feel ashamed even to use a urinal when there are other men present and will choose to use a cubicle for fear of ridicule. However, when I show them a series of photographs of different penises they are usually able to pick one out that is very similar to their own. Yet these pictures are of regular, normal penises.

Figure 1
Illustration of uncircumcised (A) and circumcised (B) penises.

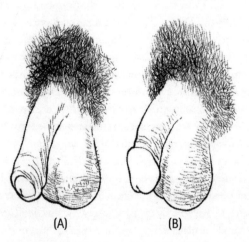

(A)   (B)

Some penises are very small in their flaccid state and some are very large, but when they become erect there is usually very little variation – an average erect penis measures five to six inches. When a man looks at his own penis, he is looking straight down at it, which causes him to get a foreshortened effect; whereas when he looks at other guys, in the changing room or shower, he is looking from a different angle and inevitably thinks that they are bigger than him. Also an uncircumcised penis will look totally different to a circumcised one, as the foreskin will cause the penis to be shaped differently.

With regard to intercourse and the penis, it is important to bear in mind that women have very little sensitivity inside the vagina and so do not really feel very much while the penis is in there. Anyway the vagina lengthens and widens to accommodate whatever size of penis goes into it, in order to provide a nice hugging feeling for it. So size really does not matter. However, *how* the penis is used matters very much.

Anatomy of the genital area

There is a small slit at the tip of the penis through which the urine flows and through which the ejaculate spurts when the man reaches orgasm or 'comes'. This opening is rather sensitive and should be treated with care. Most of the man's sensitivity is at the tip, or glans, of the penis as there are lots of nerve endings in the glans and so stimulation of this area is immensely pleasurable. This is also why intercourse is so satisfying for the male as he has all those nerve endings being enclosed by the warm and well-lubricated vagina.

At the end of the glans is a ridge called the coronal ridge and, in an uncircumcised male, the foreskin is attached to this ridge. Particular attention should be paid to hygiene regarding the foreskin and, from an early age, boys should be taught to pull the foreskin back and wash the penis. This prevents what is called smegma from building up. Smegma is a cheesy-like substance that is not only very off-putting in lovemaking but can also lead to inflammation and infection. In most cases there is usually no need for circumcision (removing the foreskin) as the foreskin retracts readily, particularly if the man has been doing this regularly since childhood. However, if there is difficulty in pulling back the foreskin or if there is any pain on retraction, it should be checked out medically.

What he likes

Men also like having attention paid to the testicles, or scrotum, in the form of kissing, sucking or licking. (I just read a great quotation from the actress Patricia Arquette, "Things you'll never hear a woman say: 'My, what an attractive scrotum!'") However, the scrotum is particularly sensitive to pain, so go warily. The scrotum contains the testicles or 'balls'. There are two testicles and this is where the sperm, which have been manufactured in the epididymis, are stored. The testicles hang outside the body in order to keep the sperm at the correct temperature, which is why the scrotum sometimes seems a bit larger and less wrinkly than at other times. This is nature doing its job of protecting the sperm.

Another area where men are particularly sensitive is the area between the scrotum and the rectum, called the perineum, and great sensations can be produced by stroking, rubbing or licking this area. Some men also derive immense pleasure from their bottom being stroked as well.

The penis itself needs attention, of course. The skin on the penis is very sensitive and fine. Large veins can be seen through the skin and this is normal, as the penis has a lot of spongy tissue that becomes engorged with blood when arousal occurs. The penis is very cunningly shaped – more or less straight on top and curved underneath – thereby facilitating a perfect fit into the curved vagina.

To give what is called 'a hand job', the woman has to be guided by the man as to how he likes her to hold his penis – after all, he has had much more experience of handling his own penis than she has. There are loads of different ways for a woman to use her hands on the penis; for instance rubbing it between her hands, using the fingertips to cause a fluttering sensation, pulling it gently towards her and letting it spring back – she should just use her imagination and have fun.

If a woman wants to produce a lot of friction with her hand then it is very effective to hold the penis as shown in *Figure 2*. Using her finger pads and thumb, she should move her hand quickly up and down in short quick strokes. She shouldn't worry, the penis can take much more pressure than she might think would be comfortable and she should probably go much quicker than she might think. Men usually say that their partners are inevitably surprised at just how much friction they require.

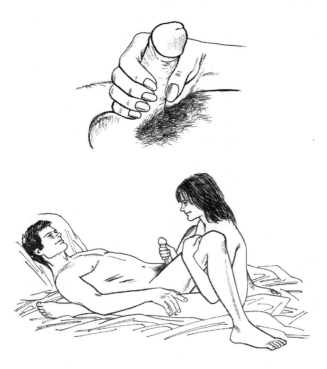

Figure 2
Rubbing Penis
If you are doing this sort of stimulation then be sure to be very comfortable yourself – two good positions are shown in *Figures 3* and *4*.

Figure 3
Hand Job
Position 1.

Figure 4
Hand Job
Position 2.

Other parts of the body can also be used to stimulate the penis, particularly the breasts. Putting the penis between the breasts (see *Figure 5*) and squeezing the breasts together produces wonderful results, and the woman can very easily either play with the penis with her fingers or kiss or lick the glans of the penis while she is doing this. The woman's hair is another form of stimulation, particularly if it is long (the hair, not the penis!) as she can gently rub it over the penis in a tantalising manner. In fact any part of the female body can be used. All that is needed is for the couple to be relaxed and inventive and the fun should follow.

Figure 5
Penis and breasts.

Erections

A man, especially a young man, can become aroused very easily and one of the first signs of his arousal is that his penis starts to become erect. Penises get erect in two stages: semi-erect and then fully erect, and this state can vary quite a lot. In other words, a man does not remain permanently erect during any one session. He can be aroused by touch, by visual stimulation and by words or a combination of all three. His erection is caused by a rush of blood to the penis causing it to grow. (Indeed the actor and comedian Robin Williams has been quoted as saying: "The problem is that God gives men a brain and a penis, and only enough blood to run one at a time." So even men contribute to their own bad press.)

During the arousal process, a number of changes happen within the male. His breathing becomes more rapid, his heartbeat and blood pressure increase, in some cases his nipples become erect and his penis begins to get erect. As he continues to be stimulated, his penis becomes even firmer and his testicles are drawn up towards his body.

Ejaculation

The next step for him is ejaculation and this happens in two stages. The first is the feeling that he is about to come – what is called *the point of inevitability* – and then the actual ejaculation. Even though it may seem that there is an awful lot of ejaculate, in fact there is quite a small amount; about a teaspoonful. A friend of mine was asked to give a semen sample and he kept on putting different samples into the little plastic container. He felt that the amount he was ejaculating was far too small and he would have been too embarrassed to hand it in to the hospital. So what they got from him ultimately was the result of a few separate attempts all put together.

Alex Comfort in his great book *The Joy of Sex* (Quartet Books Ltd, London, 1996) suggests that if the guy wants to increase the amount of ejaculate he should masturbate *almost* to orgasm about an hour before he makes love. In this way he increases the prostate secretion, which contributes to the overall ejaculation.

Every seventy days the sperm are replaced with fresh ones, which explains why men can father healthy children until the end of their lives. Women on the other hand are born with a certain number of eggs that are not replaced as they die off.

After ejaculation, the penis becomes semi-erect and then flaccid and it will be some time before the man can become erect again or ejaculate. Gradually a man's heartbeat, blood pressure and penis are back where they started and often he will feel quite sleepy due to seratonin being released in his brain – so, on the 'once they are satisfied they roll over and go to sleep' front, he really does have an excuse.

Oral sex

As we are looking at the arousal process in men, I think this is a good time to talk about oral sex which, when administered to a man, is called fellatio. Oral sex is a topic that comes up very often in therapy and, over the years, I have reached my own conclusions about it. It seems to me that the person that benefits the most from oral sex is the receiver, which is why it seems only fair that it is a two-way process. A lot of women say that, while they absolutely love receiving oral sex, they have great reservations about giving it. This seems to be unfair because if you are willing to receive then you should be willing to give. Moreover, as practically all the women I have spoken to become highly aroused through oral sex, it is in their own interests to give it as well as to receive it.

After further questioning, women have two main concerns: that the penis is not very clean and that the man will ejaculate in her mouth.

The cleanliness issue can be dealt with by personal hygiene. It really doesn't take very long to ensure a clean penis – it takes a lot longer to give enough oral sex for a man to ejaculate! If the woman has concerns about these two matters then the way to deal with it is for her to say what is, and is not, acceptable.

Often women say they are afraid they are not any good at oral sex. I do not believe there is any such thing as being bad at any form of sex. There is only finding out what works for the couple – what was really good with a previous partner will probably not have the same effect with the current one. This is what makes it all such fun, every sexual encounter is unique to the couple involved. And, women, if you have any worries about not being good at giving oral sex, think 'ice cream cone' – your partner will really enjoy you working your way through that ice cream!

[3]

THE AROUSAL
PROCESS IN
WOMEN

Women! How often I have heard that word said in exasperation, almost with an exclamation mark after it. "Women! I will never understand them!" Indeed women sometimes can be difficult to understand if you are a man, as they appear to be more complicated than men. There is an awful lot going on inside their heads that is unsaid, whereas men, on the whole, are much more straightforward and direct. There are a lot of differences between men and women and nowhere is this imbalance as apparent as in the genital area. If you look at a woman, all you see is pubic hair with not a hint of what is going on inside or of all the delights that are possible. Yet, with the male, the penis is in full view, flaccid or erect – what you see is what you get.

Indeed, when comparing the two in the arousal process, it is useful to make an analogy with the world of cookery: think of the woman as an electric cooker and the man as a gas one. When you put a kettle of water on an electric plate it takes quite a while to come to the boil – although it does get there in the end – and, if you were to keep the kettle on the plate even after the electricity has been turned off, it would continue to simmer away for some time. Put the same kettle on the gas and it boils up much more quickly, but when the gas is turned off there is very little heat left in the burner soon afterwards.

Arousal

Let us look at the arousal process in a woman. The first thing that happens when a woman begins to get aroused is that her nipples become erect. For most women, breasts are an erogenous zone and a woman can become quite aroused if her breasts are massaged, rubbed, sucked or kissed by her partner. But she responds best when the touching is little and often – a form of teasing – as too much of anything is boring. (This applies to her other erogenous zones, as well.) For some women, however, breasts are not at all sensitive.

For most women, breasts come in two sizes – too big or too small. Those with big breasts complain that they have to take the wrong size in clothes to accommodate them, they make them feel self-conscious, they jump around too much when they are jogging/running for the bus/taking part in sports and they are often just plain uncomfortable, as the weight of the breasts is out of proportion to their body size.

Those with small breasts, on the other hand, long for a cleavage and feel that they would have a much better sex life and more success with men if they had bigger breasts. In my experience, men generally accept the breasts as part of the woman they are with, even if they do have a preference for one particular type of breast. I have never heard a man say that he does not fancy a woman because of her big or small breasts, and yet they are a source of constant unhappiness for a large number of women.

Anatomy of the genital area

Now we come to the genital area, so let's have a guided tour for both men and women who do not know their way around.

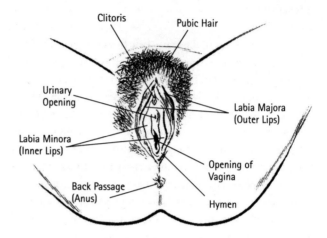

Figure 6
The female
genital area.

I am constantly surprised by the number of women who have never even looked at their own genital area and yet those same women can describe in great detail any other part of their anatomy.

In order for a woman to see her vulval area she has to use a mirror, so perhaps inaccessibility adds to the general mystique surrounding it. The entire area is covered in pubic hair, often in the shape of a triangle although in some women it extends right up towards the waist and onto the tops of the legs.

Different women have different attitudes to pubic hair. Some women keep it very short, some shave it all off (although re-growth can be ticklish) and, in some cases, it can cause real problems. Such was the case with a young client of mine who was terribly hung up on the fact that she was a true redhead and so her pubic hair was also red. She felt that this would be a real turn-off for men and she could not ever allow them to see her naked. We had long discussions about her pubic hair and what she could do about it before she was able to move forward in therapy. Her problem had been exacerbated by having been asked in a teasing way by a young neighbour, when she was only ten, if she had a 'red pussy'. She replied that they only had a dog, and was absolutely mortified some years later when she fully understood the question.

Underneath the pubic hair is the pubic bone and this is an important part of the female anatomy, as it covers her clitoris, which we will come to very shortly. When the male pubic bone rubs against the female one during intercourse, it produces very intense sensations. Indeed these sensations do not only occur during intercourse – we can probably all remember early experiences when, even without undressing, very pleasurable sensations were produced by rubbing against another person and making pubic bone contact.

OUTER AND INNER LIPS

The female genital area is made up of the labia majora (the outer lips) and, inside these, the labia minora (the inner lips). When a woman is aroused, there is a rush of blood to her entire genital area that causes these lips to expand and enlarge. This is nature's way of ensuring that she is on the way to being prepared to have intercourse. Nature's main intention is that procreation happens and so the whole arousal process revolves around that eventuality. In other words, the body responds to arousal so that there is a maximum chance of a pregnancy occurring, even though, for various other reasons (including birth control) there may be no possibility of a pregnancy.

Very shortly after the woman begins to get aroused, natural lubrication starts to occur in the vagina. The reason for the lubrication is to make intercourse pleasurable – if the vagina is dry it can be painful. Along with the natural lubrication that occurs it can be helpful, especially in the early stages of lovemaking, to use some other form as well. The most obvious is the man's saliva, but sometimes this is not enough and some form of lubricant should be used if necessary – there are lots of different ones available, such as KY Jelly, Astraglide or Sylk.

VAGINA

The vagina is the canal that runs between the womb and the vulval area and it is located behind the inner lips. It has an opening that is not immediately visible, as the walls of the vagina lie against each other. Around the same time as lubrication begins, the vagina starts to widen and lengthen and the womb starts to move upwards, all of which will enable the penis to have lots of room when there is penetration.

The word I keep coming back to is 'arousal' and it is very important that the woman is aroused before there is any attempt at penetration. If we go back to the electricity and gas analogy we can see that the man is ready for penetration as soon as he has an erection, but it may take the women fifteen to twenty minutes before she is ready, so obviously the man has to be very aware of this and not penetrate too soon.

CLITORIS

Although lubrication takes place in the vagina, almost all the woman's feelings of arousal emanate from the clitoris, which is a tiny organ, about half the size of a fingernail, situated well above the vaginal opening. If he were to do nothing else, the man should make the acquaintance of his partner's clitoris and discover how she likes it to be treated. No two women are the same but the clitoris is an incredibly sensitive little button and should, therefore, be handled with care. Indeed, when a woman is highly aroused, a little hood comes down over the clitoris and the man may have difficulty in locating it (see *Figure 6* on *page 36*).

The stimulation of the clitoris, either directly using the fingers or tongue, or indirectly through intercourse will bring a woman to climax, i.e. to orgasm. While the sensation of being penetrated is extremely pleasurable for a woman, the majority of her sensitive nerve endings are in the clitoris, which is why she can have really enjoyable sex without having intercourse. Indeed, since most women masturbate using their hand or an object, such as a vibrator, to stimulate the area around the clitoris, without any form of penetration, you can see what an important role it plays in the arousal process.

There are of course lots of other erogenous zones for a woman. The inner thighs are very sensitive in a lot of women and they can get very turned on by slow stroking of these. Also the buttocks can respond to stimulation, either in the form of squeezing, licking, gentle biting or sucking. A couple I know used to do a lot of 'bum biting' and derived great pleasure and a lot of laughs from it. Some women also respond to slapping of the buttocks and it is up to each person to discover what works for their partner. Go gently at first – you can always increase the strength later. Experimenting with positions in order to give maximum access to buttocks and breasts can add a lot to the sexy feeling you are trying to create.

Do not forget kissing. I always ask my clients about kissing and more often than not it does not exist anymore apart from the cursory peck. But think back to the very early teens or the very beginning of a relationship and you can be sure that great heights of arousal were reached just with kissing. Remember those nights in steamed up cars? Or in the back row at the cinema? Most of us can remember our first kiss as clearly as our first intercourse, and that surely says a lot about kissing. So whenever in doubt, kiss. And then kiss again. And after that, don't forget to kiss. Results guaranteed.

Oral sex

Cunnilingus, the official title given to oral sex when applied to women, is often another great means of arousal. Some men, and indeed some women, have some problems with it and the most common of these is in the area of hygiene. At different times of her cycle, a woman will have different secretions and may be very conscious of these. She may, therefore, feel disinclined to be that intimate with her partner. Or he may have reservations of his own regarding smell or taste. A shower or, if that is not possible, a wash of the genital area is a must as far as I am concerned in order for both partners to feel good.

This does not mean that there is anything wrong with a woman's individual smell. In fact, that individual smell can be very erotic. I remember a male client speaking very wistfully of a previous girlfriend's vaginal secretions and what a powerful aphrodisiac they were for him. He told me that he had driven from Galway to Dublin one time after visiting her and he had reminded himself of the great sex they had by sniffing his fingers. This made the car journey much shorter for him.

What the man does regarding oral sex is up to him, but it is a great help if the woman can let him know that what he is doing feels good – encouragement is a great morale booster from his point of view. Women are generally inclined to think that the man should just know without being told about all manner of things but, in sex especially, it is important that you do tell him what pleases you.

If the man is going to spend some time on giving his partner oral sex then he should be sure that he is comfortable and should find a position that suits them both. While giving oral sex he should be sure to use his hands as well so that, while he is licking or probing with his tongue, his hands can be playing with her breasts or buttocks. Also he can use his hands on the outer and inner lips to rub and stroke while using a light flicking movement with his tongue. Remember that action *around* the clitoris rather than actually on it is far more pleasurable for a woman. If a man uses a circular motion with his head while giving oral sex it can be very arousing for her.

The G-spot

The jury still appears to be out regarding the 'G-spot'. Some people say it does exist; others that it does not. It seems to me that some women *do* have an area inside the vagina that is particularly sensitive. It is extremely difficult for a woman to check this out for herself, so if a couple wants to investigate it, this is what they should do. The female lies on her back with her legs apart. With the palm of his hand facing upward the man gently inserts his well-lubricated index or third finger into her vagina, moves it a little to the right and makes a 'come here' motion with his finger. By moving his finger in this way his fingertip should touch her G-spot (see *Figure 7*).

The only thing to be aware of is that the woman may feel the need to urinate and so, before attempting this, she should have an empty bladder. Then when she feels like urinating she knows that she does not need to and the feeling passes after a few moments. Sometimes G-spot stimulation and clitoral stimulation combined can lead to an intense orgasm. A lot of women do not appear to have a G-spot but it is worth giving it a try – just make sure that his nails are well trimmed before starting the investigation.

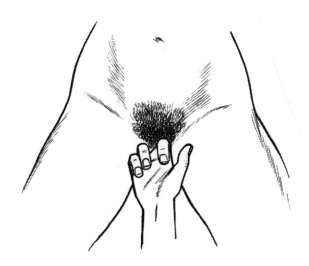

Figure 7
Diagram of finger in vagina.

As a woman becomes more and more excited, her breathing gets faster, her heartbeat increases, her blood pressure rises and she experiences a building up of tension that finally gets released as an orgasm and she 'comes'. This is accompanied by a feeling of tremendous relaxation and peacefulness. Whatever the man is doing as he senses she is moving close to orgasm he should continue until he is told to stop, as it is very easy for her to go off the boil and not reach a climax. He will know when she has climaxed as women will generally make some sort of sound during orgasm – some very loud, some just a little peep – and afterwards she will just want to be held for a while.

For a woman it is possible to go on and have further orgasms very quickly and, in this, women differ from men.

Words are a great aphrodisiac and if you saw Jane Fonda in the film *Klute* (1971) you will know what I mean. It is great for a woman to be told that her lover finds her sexy and be told about the things that he likes in her. In particular, a woman likes to hear good things about the bits that she is unsure of, and if her partner knows her at all, he will know where she needs reassurance. So he should tell her he finds such things as her breasts, her legs, her underwear, her very wetness a turn-on and this in turn helps to get her more turned on herself. Arousal is all about getting lost in the moment and forgetting about everyday things, and the more that can be done in this regard the better. I object to the term 'talking dirty', so how about 'talking sexily' instead?

I have concentrated on the obvious physical sources of pleasure for a woman, but it is important to realise that mentally a woman responds to all sorts of other things as well, even little things, and things that are done and said away from the bedroom are as important as the actual physical act. A telephone call to see how she is doing, an offer to help with a chore, a morning cup of tea if you are sharing a home, an unexpected bunch of flowers or bar of chocolate – all manner of things can be just as important as sex for making her feel wanted and desired. So foreplay should be an ongoing thing and not just something that lasts for a short time before getting on with the sexual act. The old notion of 'wham, bam, thank you, mam' is by now extinct, I hope.

[4]

COMMON
DIFFICULTIES
FOR MEN

Erectile dysfunction

The best thing that has happened to men for a long time has got to be Viagra. Not just because they now have another option to help with erections but because it has made it acceptable to at least talk openly about the problem. I know in a lot of cases the whole Viagra saga has been treated as a joke but, underneath all that, it was tremendously freeing for men to discover that they were not alone and that literally hundreds of thousands of other men also suffered from erectile difficulties. More than six million prescriptions were written for Viagra in the first eight months it was on the market. I know from my own practice that men are a bit more comfortable now in admitting that they do have problems and that they want to do something about them. People usually assume that it is the women who seek out help in the first instance and they are very surprised when I tell them that at least 50 per cent of my first-time clients are men on their own. Their ages vary from twenty to late seventies and I have great admiration for them for doing something about their problems – after all it is more difficult for men to talk than it is for women.

I have yet to meet a man who has not had problems with erections at some stage in his life. There can be many different reasons – tiredness, overuse of alcohol or drugs, anxiety, fancying the woman too much, fear of pregnancy, guilt because he is being unfaithful to his current partner… the list is endless. The trouble is that, unlike women, who will not get too worried if they have a few lovemaking experiences in a row without an orgasm, men get very anxious very quickly. After which they start watching out for it to happen – this is called 'spectatoring' – and, of course, when they do that, men stop being aroused and the whole thing goes flat! Men have come in to see me who have had two 'bad' experiences in a row and have been convinced that it is all over and they are going to have difficulties with erections from now on. And I suppose to a certain extent that is true because, if they believe that they are going to have problems, it can become a self-fulfilling prophecy.

So the number one rule when you encounter difficulties is to *relax.* This, of course, applies in so many areas of our lives and yet we find it so difficult. If you are taking up a new sport like golf you will be told endless times to relax, if you are about to make a speech and are nervous you will be told to relax, if you are getting hot under the collar about other drivers when you are in your car, chances are somebody in the car will suggest that you relax. I know it is difficult at times to relax but I believe that we all should find something that works for us to enable us to relax. If I had a pound for every time that work stress is mentioned in my clinic I could retire. And I honestly do not believe that it was as bad as this for previous generations where life was lived at a much more leisurely pace. So much for the Celtic Tiger!

The first thing that a man should do if he is having difficulties with erections is to have himself checked out medically. This was brought home to me very forcibly a number of years ago when Joe, who was having problems, came to see me. He was in his early seventies and had been widowed for two years, but for a number of years prior to his wife's death they had not been sexually active. He had now started a new relationship and was delighted with how things were going except for the fact that he could not get an erection. He was very anxious to move on to being fully sexual and so was his new partner. He supposed that it was lack of use and his advancing years that were to blame, but decided to check it out anyway. As a result of a newspaper advertisement, he had gone to a clinic where they suggested some penile injections (this was in the pre-Viagra days). However, they said that due to his age they could not guarantee that the injections would continue to work and yet they charged him £350 and sent him off. The injections worked partially for a short time. When he came to see me I asked that he get checked out medically, before I went any further with counselling him, and put him in touch with an urologist. The urologist subsequently discovered a tumour that necessitated surgery and I felt very angry indeed with those people who were out to make a fast buck.

In telling this story I do not want to be alarmist and the fact is that most of the men that I refer for medical checks come back with a clean bill of health. I am just suggesting that this is the route to begin with. As a general rule, if you are getting morning erections and are functioning well in masturbation then it is most likely that your problems are psychological, but get it checked out anyway. Go to your GP and they will most likely run some tests, such as checking for diabetes and checking your testosterone level. In some cases your GP will then refer you to an urologist, the male equivalent of a gynaecologist.

Below are a few different case histories that will illustrate for you some examples of how men can encounter difficulties with erections.

■ **Cathy and Tony** came to see me as they had not as yet consummated their marriage. After taking a detailed history, it was revealed that Tony had grown up in an all female

46

household, as he was an only boy and his father had died when he was very young. His older sisters and mother all protected and nurtured Tony who was not only the only son but the youngest in the family. He had matured into a really lovely, gentle person but had been so protected that he had very little knowledge of the real world and had not had any real girlfriends before Cathy. She also was inclined to take care of him and mother him, which suited him very well.

When we were discussing his previous sexual history, which of course was very scant, he told me of an incident that had upset him profoundly. He had been out with a friend and they had ended up in a nightclub attached to a hotel. There he had been chatted up by a woman who was a good deal older and much more experienced than he was. She was staying in the hotel and, after a few hours in his company, she invited him up to her room. When they got there, and after a very short time just kissing, she told him to take his clothes off and handed him a condom with instructions to put it on. Now, as he had never even been naked with anybody before, let alone used a condom, you can imagine how terrifying all of this was for him. When he had taken his clothes off and, after some time, was still not getting an erection, she was rather disparaging towards him, whereupon he left feeling absolutely shattered. This one event affected his confidence to such an extent that, even though he loved Cathy very much, he was hugely anxious every time they tried to make love.

■ **Ruth and Louis** had been married for five years and had known each other since their early teens – they were now both thirty. He ran his own very successful business and she was a self-employed designer. She had initiated their coming to see me as she was at her wits end as to what to do. They never made love anymore whereas at the beginning of their relationship it had been wonderful. She wasn't asking for the level that they had at the beginning, but this beautiful young

SEXUAL HEALING

woman found no lovemaking at all simply unacceptable. Louis
was also very unhappy with how things were, but cited pressure
of work as being the reason and, indeed, he did work very hard
with frequent but brief periods away from home.

When I started to unravel things with them, I discovered
that Louis had been in business with his father and when his
father died things had begun to go wrong. For a long time he
was both grieving the death of a beloved father and trying to
keep the business going and, as a result, had started to have
erectile difficulties. He felt bad about this, particularly as he
wanted things to be good for Ruth who was tremendously
supportive throughout this time. He reported how he started
to stay up late rather than go to bed with her because she
might want to make love. And if they did go to bed at the
same time he would have a huge knot in his stomach from
tension about what was to come.

Also Ruth's body clock was beginning to tick and she wanted
to start a family, which added another huge stress. How could
she make a baby when her partner had difficulties having, or
maintaining, an erection?

■ **Sean** was a big, tall, handsome, farmer's son who had never
had a long-term girlfriend. He suffered from depression and
was on medication for that condition and he also suffered
from irritable bowel syndrome. His libido had suffered as a
result of the medication and he had difficulties having an
erection. When he first came to see me, he was generally very
anxious and very down. I had his medication changed to an
anti-depressant that does not affect libido and that helped
greatly with his sexual appetite. However, there was no great
improvement on his erectile difficulties and, to crown it all, he
was now experiencing premature ejaculation on the odd occasion
when he was with a girl. His opinion of himself was very
low which contributed to his lack of success in even chatting
up women.

■ **Aisling and Pat** had been married for five years, when she was referred to me by her GP suffering from vaginismus, meaning she was unable to have intercourse. Aisling and Pat attended the clinic together for treatment and it became apparent that their relationship was incredibly stormy. She had a particularly strong temper and raged at him quite a bit for all sorts of things, including his lack of success with erections. She did, indeed, suffer with vaginismus and he did, indeed, have erectile difficulties but an awful lot of *his* problems were to do with the bad state of their relationship and her habit of constantly putting him down. In this instance, relationship counselling had to be undergone before any attempt was made at psychosexual therapy.

■ **Ray** came to see me on his own. He and his girlfriend had been together for about two years and she attended his graduation ball with him. This was the night he decided that they should finally consummate the relationship and she was willing. Unfortunately, he decided to do this having first consumed eight pints of beer. Ray was about 5'2" and fairly slight, so that much beer had quite an effect on him. When the time came to have sex he had no erection whatsoever.

His girlfriend did not make any fuss and treated the whole thing fairly lightly. But already the warning bells were starting to go off in his head, particularly as he had never previously had intercourse. Shortly afterwards they went abroad to visit some friends of hers and she spent the entire time chatting up a particularly good-looking guy in their group and excluding Ray. By the time they returned he was totally lacking in confidence and although he could get an erection, he lost it any time he tried for penetration. When he came to see me the relationship was over, but he was becoming increasingly anxious about any future relationship and how he was going to cope when the time came for him to be fully sexual.

What can be done about erection difficulties?

So you are having erection problems. What can you do and what are the options open to you? Now as I said already, the first thing to do is relax. Among all the options open to you something is going to be right for you and you are going to get back to functioning properly. So stop being so hard on yourself and think positively – it's going to be ok.

Firstly, if you are in a relationship, have a good look at that and consider whether it could be contributing to your problem. If so, talk this through with your partner and seek some counselling to help make things better between you. If your relationship is not the problem, there are a number of medical interventions open to you.

VIAGRA

As I have mentioned already, Viagra is now readily available through your doctor and works for about 70 per cent of men. Those men for whom it is working are full of praise for it, particularly at how natural the whole procedure is. A pill is taken and between thirty and forty-five minutes later – providing they have some form of stimulation, either visual or physical – an erection happens. The effect lasts for four or five hours and a lot of my clients would report equal satisfaction the following morning. (A plea here on behalf of the partners – if you have a regular partner then do discuss taking Viagra with them. A number of women reported very mixed feelings when their partners started to use Viagra as they were being called on to be sexual at a rate that was far above what they were used to and without much consideration being given to their feelings.)

Viagra does have some reported side effects such as headaches, flushing, indigestion and, in a very small percentage, some vision problems, such as a blue tinge or blurred vision. There have also been a small number of deaths and Viagra is not prescribed to men who have angina or who are on medication to control blood pressure or on any drugs containing nitrates. It is also quite expensive. In an ideal world, I would like to see Viagra used as a bridge whereby a man will use it to build his confidence and then gradually dispense with it, for instance, using it every second time and gradually weaning himself off it. Some of my clients use it for special occasions where they are going away for the weekend or on holidays and want to experience longer-than-usual sessions or do not want to have to worry about maintaining an erection.

I suppose this is using it as a recreational drug for a bit of a treat.

UPRIMA

This is a new pill that has come on the market and has the same effect as Viagra, but works more quickly. Check with your doctor which would be the most suitable for you.

YOHIMBINE

This is a drug that also comes in pill form and is made from the bark of an African tree. It has not had anything like the success rate of Viagra – 20 per cent as opposed to 70 per cent – but the side effects are very mild. They include a slight headache and a small increase in blood pressure, but it may be worth trying if your doctor suggests it.

INJECTION THERAPY

This consists of the man injecting himself into the side of the penis with a drug that helps to relax the smooth muscles and arteries of the penis and, therefore, increases the blood supply. It was the main option open to men before Viagra and is very successful. The GP firsts shows the patient how to administer the injection to begin with and also determines what dosage is right for him. From then on, the man can do it himself. An erection follows in quite a short time and will last for about forty-five minutes.

The obvious disadvantage is the injection itself and some people find it painful, although an auto-injector can help. Also, there is a small risk of priapism, where the erection will not go down, and this then needs to be treated either by your doctor or in a hospital emergency room. All of this will be explained to you when you discuss this option with your doctor. In cases where Viagra does not work, injection therapy very often does, so it will remain as a second-line treatment.

VACUUM DEVICES

Vacuum pumps are another option and some men choose them because they are totally non-invasive. A plastic cylinder fits over the penis and a lever is pressed that pumps the air out of the cylinder creating a vacuum which draws blood into the penis thereby creating an erection. A constricting ring is placed at the base of the penis, which keeps it erect, and the vacuum pump is then removed. I have found that some diabetic men like to use this device, as they do not want to put any chemicals into their bodies. Also, some men who have erectile dysfunction due to prostate surgery favour pumps.

They are quite clumsy to look at and require both a sense of humour and an understanding partner, and some report that the constricting ring can be painful, but they are well worth investigating and those who are happy with them speak very highly of them.

PENILE IMPLANTS

There is a surgical procedure whereby some form of silicon rods is inserted into the penis. Then, either manually or with the aid of a pump, it is possible to achieve an erection. Obviously this involves full surgery and is not contemplated lightly, but it is an important option, particularly for those for whom the other treatments are not possible. It is also irreversible and, from what I have seen on film, the penis looks different after the operation, in that the top is less rigid than the rest of the erect penis. Obviously very detailed discussion with the urologist would be necessary before such a step is considered.

These are the medical interventions that are open to you. However, bear in mind that an awful lot of your problems are in your own head and, if you can learn to gain sufficient confidence in your erectile ability, you may not need to use anything else.

Exercises

EXERCISES FOR YOU ONLY
In order to help build your confidence there are some exercises that you can undertake. The first few exercises I would like you to do on your own and then, if you have a partner, you can get her to read what is suggested and see if she would be willing to help. More about that later (see *pages 56-61*).

You must set some time aside on a regular basis to do all these exercises. If you are learning to drive or learning something like golf then you will take regular lessons and that is how you achieve results. The same is true with these exercises. If it is a case of only now and again then you really will not get very far and you will become disheartened with your lack of progress. So, make some time for yourself twice a week, with at least a day between each exercise.

Make sure you are not pushed for time, and that you can put on the answering machine and turn off the mobile phone. Choose a time when you are not feeling too tired – so not last thing at night. Start each session with a bath or a shower as this will help to energise and to relax. Play some background music that is fairly gentle and do not have too bright a light – a bedside light or candles would be ideal.

Make sure that all these things have been taken care of before every session so that you are as relaxed as possible when you start your exercises.

Exercise One

Lie on your bed in a warm room and begin to breathe deeply and continue to do this until you have a breathing rhythm established. Then start to focus on your body – in other words start to think about what sensations are produced as you start to touch your body.

It helps to get used to touching your body if you use some sort of lotion as you gently stroke your body. Men are not used to using lotions on their bodies unless it is after sunbathing, but you should start, as it is beneficial to your skin and also gets you used to touching your body. Gently stroke the bits that you can easily get at – your tummy, chest and arms. You will feel a bit strange in the beginning, but never mind, you will get used to it.

When you are comfortable doing this, then move on to touching the penis and genital area. You are not trying to produce an erection, but you are trying to discover, or rediscover, what sort of touch produces a good feeling for you.

Then put a lubricant on both hands and experiment with that to find out what sort of touch feels arousing. Experiment with different strokes and touches, light and heavy, fast and slow and just relax and enjoy the touch. If you find you are starting to get an erection just experience the sensation but don't do anything with it.

Remember you are not trying to produce an erection, just experimenting with touch and what is pleasurable for you. Do this for about ten minutes.

This exercise should be repeated two more times on two separate occasions, some days apart, before you move on to Exercise Two.

COMMON DIFFICULTIES FOR MEN

Exercise Two

Now touch your penis with a lubricated hand in one of the ways that you know feels good. Then, either by having an accompanying fantasy in your head or by looking at a stimulating picture, continue the movement until you get an erection. This will happen naturally if you have set the scene and are relaxed – after all, an erection is what happens when there is a rush of blood to the penis when you are aroused, and you get aroused either by touch or mental stimulation. So don't worry, it will happen.

When it does, stop whatever you have been doing to produce this erection and it will start to go away. Wait until you are semi-erect – it may take a few minutes or just a few seconds – and then start all over again. Repeat this for a third time and the exercise is finished. (If you want, at this stage, to go on to ejaculation then that is all right – I would hate to see you frustrated.) The ejaculation stage is unimportant, but what is very important is for you to see that erections come and go; there will be another one along shortly, just like the 15B bus! Repeat this exercise during two further sessions, leaving some days in between each session, until you are confident that you have grasped this concept.

If you are finding difficulty in getting the erection, or regaining it, just check out that you have all the things in place for getting aroused. Are you relaxed? Are you breathing deeply? Are you turning your mind over fully to the fantasy you are creating in your head or the visual material you are using? If you feel you are doing all of this and nothing is happening, then call it a day for the moment and start again next time. Quite often it takes a few sessions for a man to be relaxed enough and confident enough within himself for things to move forward. This is quite natural, as anything new feels a bit strange to begin with.

Exercise Three

Now that you are confident with getting and maintaining erections, there is still a very beneficial exercise that you can do, even if you have no partner. This involves following Exercise Two until you have the erection established and then starting to focus on where things have gone wrong in the past.

It is often upon entering the vagina or just afterwards that the erection starts to wane. So imagine that this is happening and plan what you are going to do to change things. Perhaps you will concentrate on your partner and the things about her body that you really love and spend some time on them. Or talk out loud about what you really like doing with her – this 'talking sexily' – sometimes gets people more turned on than they would normally be. Or maybe you would like to either give or receive oral sex.

You should concentrate on doing, in your mind, whatever is your particular fancy, while continuing on with the physical touching that you like to do on your penis. If you give yourself over completely to the fantasy of what you would like to do with your partner, you will find that it is having the desired effect on your penis. If it is not happening, then ask yourself – are you relaxed, are you totally immersed in what you are doing or are you still worrying about the firmness of your erection?

You will find that after a few times – and the number of times varies with different people – things will start to happen. When they do, continue on in your fantasy to a successful conclusion.

EXERCISES WITH A PARTNER
First of all plan your sessions. It sounds a bit clinical and indeed it is a bit clinical, but that way you ensure you have regular sessions, you make progress and no hidden agendas creep

in. Aim to have a least two sessions a week, and if you can manage three that would be great.

From now until you are told otherwise, there is a ban on attempted intercourse, orgasm and ejaculation. There is no ban on masturbation to climax, except in each other's presence.

Every session should be preceded by a bath or shower. While one person showers, the other should prepare the room. Make sure it is warm, have subdued lighting, maybe light a few candles and put on some background music – answerphones should be turned on for all phones.

Exercise One

You will use this hour to give and receive massage. Divide the hour into two halves and give each other a massage devoting roughly fifteen minutes to each side of the body. However, for the moment skip the breasts, buttocks and the genital area. The purpose of the massage is to see how you like to touch your partner and to be touched by them in a non-sexual way, although you both are naked. This is called sensate focus because you are using all of the senses: seeing, hearing, taste, touch and smell. The sense of taste is covered by giving little butterfly kisses whenever you feel like it to whatever parts of the body takes your fancy, except the areas mentioned above. Vary the touch you use to see what you both like most.

Start by getting your partner to lie on their stomach with their arms stretched above their head. You then begin with their head and, taking your time, experience all the different contours of their head and hair using different strokes. Move on slowly down the back, up along the arms and massage the individual fingers. Cover the entire body in this way right down to the toes, but skip the buttocks. Then get your partner to turn over on their back and you begin again, starting with the face – don't forget the kisses. If you are a man, do not touch either the breasts or the genital area; if you are a woman, skip the genital area. We all feel more vulnerable while we are lying on our backs so be sensitive to this with your partner. After all our entire body is exposed, with all the lumps and bumps, scar marks and all the bits we may be unhappy about in full view. I ask people to do this exercise initially with just their bare hands and then to add whatever lotion or oil they like so that they can experience the difference.

Sometimes a woman is unable to allow her body to be fully exposed and in that case it is all right to use something like a scarf to cover the areas she has a problem with – usually the breasts, genital area and/or bottom – until she has got used to the whole idea of relaxing with her partner and then gradually feeling comfortable enough to remove the scarf.

At the end of each session spend a few minutes in each other's arms talking and having a cuddle and telling each other what the time was like for you. It is, after all, a very intimate exercise. You can have sex with a perfect stranger but there is no way you would give that same stranger the intimate massage that you have just shared with your partner.

Do not move on to the next exercise until you have done this exercise successfully, on three separate occasions.

Exercise Two

Having successfully completed Exercise One three times, you are now ready to move on to including the breasts and the genital area in the massage. Proceed as directed in Exercise One, but this time, touch the breast and genital areas. Remember that this is an overall massage; don't concentrate on these new areas with a view to becoming aroused.

Men, be aware that your partner will be massaging your penis and scrotum and in the past you may have become anxious whenever she got to that point, but now just relax and enjoy the sensations as you are required to do nothing at all. Lie back and enjoy it.

When you are giving the massage to your partner, you should only brush your fingers over her pubic hair without trying to be more intimate and continue on down the body. When your partner is giving you the massage, she should touch your penis in whatever way she feels like.

This is a more complete exercise than the previous one as you are touching the whole body. Again, do this exercise on three different occasions before going on to the next exercise.

Exercise Three

By now things are progressing nicely, so you are ready to move on to arousal. This involves getting aroused, but not really doing anything with it, so don't get anxious! Have the massage as before, but now concentrate on what you know you like to do and on what your partner likes you to do. When you have had a relaxing massage and are feeling good about each other, move on to a more arousing type of touch and some more passionate kissing – whatever it is that usually turns you on with each other.

At this point your partner takes over for a little while. She should stimulate the penis in whatever way she likes until you have an erection, and then she should stop doing whatever it was she was doing and let the erection subside. This is called waxing and waning and you should do this a few times before going on to ejaculation, if you feel like doing that. But only if you feel like it; it doesn't really matter whether you ejaculate or not.

It is only fair that you then help to bring the female to climax, if this is what she wants, in whatever way she likes. If, up until now, you have only achieved orgasm through intercourse, it is time to become a little more creative and experiment! Remember you have hands and a mouth – not just a penis!

Exercise Four

Move on only when you are quite confident with waxing and waning. As you can see, we move in small stages. Have the massage as before and then proceed to the next step, which is to practise the position for intercourse. Do this by spending some time with the woman on top just playing with the penis. So just imagine that the penis is a paintbrush and she is painting the labia and the entrance to the vagina. No interior decorating at this stage! Just get used to the sensation.

Exercise Five

It's time now to become a little more creative and put these steps together. Begin with the massage as usual, then move on to arousal and whatever foreplay is good for both of you. At some stage, the woman gets on top and plays with the penis for a while before she inserts it in the vagina. No movement at this stage. Just wait for the erection to subside. This, perhaps, is what used to happen in the times when you were having problems, but now this is what you are being instructed to do. And no movement *means* no movement by either of you. Frustrating as it may be, it's important that you take this stage slowly.

Exercise Six

Go through all of the previous steps but now include gentle thrusting from the female. Relax and enjoy the sensations. When you get comfortable with this, then you can go on to

COMMON DIFFICULTIES FOR MEN

some thrusting yourself and ultimately, of course, this will bring you to ejaculation.

So now you have taught yourself the necessary steps to ridding yourself of your anxieties – with a little help from your partner of course. Enjoy the benefits of your hard work.

Premature ejaculation

Premature ejaculation, or PE as it is referred to, must be one of the most frustrating conditions for any man – and, come to think of it, for any man's partner. Premature ejaculation is when a man does not have control over when he ejaculates and so this usually happens way before he wants it to. Sometimes it will happen before he even attempts intercourse, sometimes very shortly (within thirty seconds) after he begins thrusting, but it is always the ejaculation that controls the man, rather than the other way around.

In my experience there are two types of premature ejaculators. The first are men who have always suffered from the condition and whose personality seems to fit into a particular category. These individuals are inclined to rush things, finish sentences for people, are a bit anxious about things in general and somewhat lacking in self-confidence. The second type will not have had PE previously, but has it in a current relationship.

Men who have had PE all their lives are by far the larger category. I feel very strongly that, of all the dysfunctions in the male, there are often no deep psychological reasons for premature ejaculation and, apart from personality type, we, as therapists, do not seem to have much information as to why men suffer from PE. However, the good news is that it is a problem that responds exceptionally well to therapy and, if the man works hard over a period of time in learning about his body's responses, he can learn to have really good control.

I remember with great affection, Joe, who came to the clinic with PE. Joe's wife came along too. He did not fit into the type of personality I have just described and, far from lacking in self-confidence was, in fact, larger than life. He was a member of a football team and they all went to the pub once a week after training. Joe was very concerned about his PE and, while the team was having a drink together one evening, he told the assembled lads that he had, as he put it, "a fierce case of premature ejaculation" and wanted to know if anybody else in the team had it. The entire team response was to tell him to shut up; they were all sure he was fine and that nobody else had any problems of any sort. They were, of course, all highly embarrassed with Joe mentioning sexual difficulties, and you can be sure somebody else in that group had some sort of problem.

Quite often PE comes about as a result of early experiences being hurried, either in masturbation or with a woman or, indeed, both. If the man is aware that his girlfriend's parents are due home any minute while they are making out on the sofa, he is surely not going to be taking his time. Likewise, if he is masturbating, but in danger of being interrupted by either a sibling or a parent, he is not going to lose any time and, in any event, the main aim in masturbation is to ejaculate. This, of course, does not apply to everybody and some men have gone through all of these experiences many times and yet do not have PE. I'm just saying early experiences of rushing things can be a contributory factor.

I remember a couple who came to see me, as their relationship was in deep trouble. The main causes of the trouble were Peter's PE, one of the most acute cases of PE I have ever seen, and Eileen's anger at him for not having done anything about it. Their relationship was in such a bad way that we had to spend some time on it before we ever tackled the sexual problem, so a number of sessions were spent in relationship counselling. I remember his absolute despair as he related the first session of sensate focus that they had together. My instructions had been to give each other a non-sexual massage with no touching of the breasts and genital area. This they had done and when she had finished giving him the massage, having kept well within the parameters of no sexual touching, he had lain there and ejaculated. She had then revisited her anger on him for not having done anything about his condition for so long. He was utterly despondent and was afraid that he would never gain any sort of ejaculatory control. In fact he did go on to get very good control, apart from a minor blip when they had quite a long break from therapy, which just emphasised to them both the need to keep working at the problem.

It should be said here that if a man ejaculates during intercourse before the woman has had an orgasm, this is not premature ejaculation. This may seem like stating the obvious but some people have unrealistic expectations and feel that if only the man had lasted longer then the woman would also have come during intercourse. In fact, straightforward intercourse (without any additional stimulation of the clitoris by the woman's own hand, her partner's hand or tongue, or by a vibrator) only produces an orgasm for about 25 per cent of women.

What to do about premature ejaculation

As usual I first consider the medical route and there is now evidence that certain medications can help PE. These are from the anti-depressant stable, such as Prozac and Xeroxat, and work for some men if they just take a pill on the day they are going to have sex. Others need to be on the medication permanently, although usually on a lower dosage than would be necessary for depression. As with all medication there are side effects. Moreover, once you stop taking the tablets, the PE returns. So talk it over with your GP if this is the route you would like to take and be guided by them as to what is best for you. It appears that there needs to be some further experimentation before a suitable drug and dosage is found. Be aware, too, that drug therapy does not work for everybody.

Circumcision is another option. This works in quite a lot of cases – an urologist friend suggests about 60 per cent – and when you think about it, it makes sense. The foreskin protects the glans of the penis and the glans is, therefore, very sensitive. If the foreskin is removed then that will, in time, cause the glans to be less sensitive and the man will not respond so readily when he penetrates the vagina and will, therefore, take longer to ejaculate. I must say that, when I outline this option to my clients, very often they firmly cross their legs and become determined to have sex therapy rather than surgery!

PE responds really well to therapy and it has been heartening, over the years, to see clients' self-esteem grow considerably as they learn to gain better control. Below are some exercises you can do to help in this regard.

Exercises

EXERCISES FOR YOU ONLY

As with all the exercises in this book a lot of the work can be done on your own before getting together with a partner. Maybe you don't have a partner. What you are going to be doing is learning to focus on your body and its responses rather than on any of the distracting techniques you may have tried – like multiplication tables or thinking of the last football match – that simply do not work. As you learn to focus on your body, you learn to be in control of your responses and you also learn what works best for you in terms of controlling your ejaculation.

You must set some time aside on a regular basis to do all these exercises. If you are learning to drive or learning something like golf then you will take regular lessons and that is how you achieve results. The same is true with these exercises. If it is a case of only now and again then you really will not get very far and you will become disheartened with your lack of progress. So, make some time for yourself two or three times a week, with at least a day between each exercise.

Make sure you are not pushed for time, and that you can put on the answering machine and turn off the mobile phone. Choose a time when you are not feeling too tired – so not last thing at night.

Start each session with a bath or a shower as this will help to energise and to relax. Play some background music that is fairly gentle and do not have too bright a light – a bedside light or candles would be ideal. Make sure that all these things have been taken care of before every session so that you are as relaxed as possible when you start your exercises.

Exercise One

You are going to start using a technique called the stop/start technique, which was pioneered by Dr James Semans in the 1950s. This involves you coming to know your point of inevitability – which is when a man would still ejaculate even if his mother came into the room. A man who has good control of his ejaculation knows his body well enough to know when he is about to come. Because he knows the point of inevitability, he also knows the point just before this and so is able to take steps not to come, such as slowing the thrusting, changing position, doing a Kegels exercise or whatever is right for him. (A Kegels exercise is where you contract the same muscles that you would contract if you were trying to stop the flow of urine. Next time you use the bathroom, you can experiment with stopping ansd starting to see what I mean.)

A premature ejaculator does not know his point of

inevitability or, indeed, the moments just before this point and so he cannot take any steps to avert the ejaculation. Therefore, this is the next point you are going to learn about.

Start masturbating with a dry hand with just enough fantasy to get an erection. Continue stroking the penis, but focus all the time on what is going on in your body and be vigilant so that you are aware of any shift in your level of arousal. When you get to the stage of feeling that you are getting close to coming – that point of inevitability – stop masturbating immediately and allow the erection to partially subside. The feeling of getting near to coming should also subside. Then start stroking the penis again and repeat the process, continuing to focus on your body's response to the stroking.

In all, the entire exercise requires you to start/stop three times and then finally continue on to ejaculation. Your aim will be to get to about three minutes on each episode, but don't worry too much about that at the beginning; it may be much shorter. However, as you get more used to the procedure you will get to three minutes and so your whole exercise will take around twelve to fifteen minutes, including stops. And really enjoy the ejaculation when it happens, because, for the first time, you are controlling it rather than the other way around. If you have a mishap and come before you intended to, just learn from the experience and next time you try the exercise you will know to stop a little sooner. It takes time. Do have patience. You will find it helpful if you write down what happened at the end of each exercise and, in that way, you can chart your progress. When you have completed the exercise successfully on three different occasions, you are ready to move on.

Exercise Two

Repeat Exercise One but this time use a lubricant, such as KY Jelly or some oil, on your hand. This will better represent the lubricated vagina to your penis. Again, you will need to continue to focus on your body's response and not allow your mind to wander. Some men find the lubricated hand much more exciting and so have to be extra careful at this point. You will also need to have completed this exercise successfully three times before moving on.

Exercise Three

With this exercise, things are going to get a little more complicated. Now, for the first time, you can allow yourself to fantasise a little. So as you are masturbating, while still concentrating on your body's responses, imagine at the same time what it is like when you are actually making love. Chances are that you are all right while thinking of the foreplay, but when it gets to penetration your wish to ejaculate increases. So slow down and think what you would do in such a situation. You would either slow the thrusting (or get the woman to slow down if, in your imagination, she is on top), change position, or do a Kegels exercise. Kegels can be very effective in treating premature ejaculation, providing you have already learned the basic control that you have practised in the previous exercises.

So do the same thing now in masturbation – slow down, do a Kegels and think your way through the scenario. It is amazing how effective this can be in helping to build both your confidence and your control. It may be that you do not get through an entire fantasised sexual encounter in the time that you are masturbating, but that is fine. Just be sure that it is you that chooses to come rather than the ejaculate choosing.

With this exercise, as time goes on, you will find that you are easily getting to three minutes without having to stop. If this is the case, then you can begin to disregard the clock and join up the sections so it becomes one long masturbation rather than three sections. This is now very realistic and represents great progress. Well done!

Exercise Four

A further refinement is that now you allow your fantasy world to develop and you continue to masturbate but with heightened arousal in your head. Still keep focusing on the point of inevitability and make the adjustments as in Exercise Three when necessary.

If you do not have a partner then continue doing these exercises regularly. They will make a tremendous difference when you next have intercourse and, while you most probably will not be performing as well as you would wish, you will still be an awful lot better than you were. And remember, the more conscious you are of what is going on in your body the more control you will have.

EXERCISES WITH A PARTNER

If you have a long-term partner who would be happy to do some of these exercises with you, then so much the better. I would suggest that you get your partner to read through the following pages so that they get some idea of what will be expected of them. You should both be aware that the exercises are somewhat clinical and rather removed from a normal love-making environment, but what you should keep in mind is that at the end of it all there will be far more satisfactory love-making for both of you.

I feel strongly that it is always advisable for the man to do the preceding exercises on his own, even if he is going to work with a partner later. In this way, he already has some idea of what getting control is all about.

First of all, plan your sessions. It sounds a bit clinical and indeed is a bit clinical but that way you ensure you have regular sessions, you make progress and no hidden agendas creep in. Aim to have at least two sessions a week, and if you can manage three that would be great – though some days should elapse between sessions.

> *From now until you are told otherwise, there is a ban on attempted intercourse, orgasm and ejaculation. There is no ban on masturbation to climax, but not in each other's presence.*
>
> *Every session should be preceded by a bath or shower. While one person showers, the other should prepare the room. Make sure it is warm, have subdued lighting, maybe light a few candles and put on some background music – answerphones should be turned on for all phones.*

Exercise One

You will use this hour to give and receive massage. Divide the hour into two halves and give each other a massage devoting roughly fifteen minutes to each side of the body. However, for the moment skip the breasts, genital area and buttocks. The purpose of the massage is to see how you like to touch your partner and to be touched by them, but in a non-sexual way although you are both naked. This is called sensate focus because you are using all of the senses: seeing, hearing, taste, touch and smell. The taste one is covered by giving little butterfly kisses whenever you feel like it to whatever parts of the body takes your fancy, except for the areas mentioned above.

Vary the touch you are using to see what you like most. Start by getting your partner to lie on their stomach with their arms stretched above their head. You then begin at the head and, taking your time, experience all the different contours of the head and the hair using different strokes. Move on slowly down the back, up along the arms and then massage the individual fingers. Cover the entire body in this way right down to the toes, but skip the buttocks. Then get them to turn over on their back and you begin again starting with the face. Don't forget the kisses! If you are a man, do not touch the breasts or the genital area; if you are a woman, skip the genital area. We all feel more vulnerable when lying on our back, so be sensitive about this with your partner. After all, our whole body is fully exposed, with all the lumps, bumps, scar marks and the bits we may be unhappy about in full view! I ask people to do this exercise initially with just their bare hands and then to add whatever lotion or oil they like so that they can experience the difference.

Sometimes a woman is unable to allow her full body to be exposed and so it is all right to use something like a scarf to cover the areas she has a problem with – usually the breasts, genital area and/or bottom – until she has got used to the whole idea of relaxing with her partner and gradually removing the scarf.

At the end of each session, spend a few minutes in each other's arms talking and having a cuddle and telling each other what the time was like for you. It is, after all, a very intimate exercise. You can have sex with a perfect stranger but there is no way that you would give that same stranger the intimate massage you have just shared with your partner. Repeat this exercise twice more before moving on to Exercise Two.

Exercise Two

Proceed as in Exercise One, but this time include the breasts and the genital area in the massage. Be aware that the breasts and genital area in the woman are only one part of the whole picture, so please don't just go for these areas. Rather, include them as you go over the entire body from the head right down to the feet. And when you are being massaged, learn to enjoy the sensation of your partner touching your penis and scrotum, rather than getting anxious that soon you will be having intercourse and you will most likely come too quickly. As always, do this exercise three times.

Exercise Three

You are now ready to move on to arousal. Shorten the length of time for both giving and receiving the massage to allow enough time for the following. After the massage, start kissing and touching each other in a way both of you know turns you on.

The woman then takes over the work and the man lies back and enjoys it. She is going to do the stop/start technique on you and the instruction for her is to stop as soon as you tell her to. From the female perspective, make sure that you are in a comfortable position before you start the stimulation and it would be helpful if you can keep an eye on the clock. You partner will be busy concentrating on his body's responses to your touch, so you are running the show! Your aim is to stimulate his penis sufficiently to keep an erection maintained for three minutes and then stop. It may well be that he will want you to stop well before that and, if so, as soon as he signals to you to stop, do so. Allow the penis to become semi-erect and then start stimulating it again.

Do this three times and then, on the fourth, stimulate your partner to ejaculation. This will obviously require much stronger stimulation than before, so be guided by him in this. Many women seem to fear that they are being too forceful when stimulating the penis, but in fact the men usually want to have even stronger movements.

After this, if the woman feels like it, her partner should go on to bring her to orgasm with either his hand or his tongue. I have found that it is far better for the woman to wait for her orgasm until after the man has come, as the sight of her having an orgasm is usually a big turn-on for the man and doesn't help with his control.

This exercise will take some time to get to the required time of three by three minutes so please be patient and you will begin to see progress. When you have done it successfully three times you are ready to move on.

Exercise Four

Proceed as for Exercise Three, but now the woman uses a lubricant on her hand. This is easier for her and helps the man, in so far as it better represents the feeling of the vagina. Do this exercise twice more before moving on.

Exercise Five

Having completed the massage, you now move on to arousal and whatever foreplay is good for both of you. When they are both aroused, the woman does one stop/start exercise and then takes up the woman-on-top position (see *pages 167-168*) and guides the erect penis into her vagina. There should be no movement. The man should just get used to the feeling of the penis being in there. Gradually the erection subsides and the woman should lift off. Then, if they wish, they can bring each other to climax without intercourse. When you have done this exercise successfully three times you are ready to move on.

Exercise Six

This exercise is a continuation of the previous one, but the woman now begins gentle thrusting during intercourse and is guided by the man's response. As soon as he indicates that he is close to climax, she either lifts off or stops thrusting. Try both and see which suits best. During all of this, don't worry too much if the man comes when he is not supposed to. It just means he did not signal early enough to ensure that he had stopped before the point of inevitability. Do not be disheartened. Almost everybody has mishaps at this stage. Do this exercise on two subsequent occasions before moving on to Exercise Seven.

Exercise Seven

Having completed the massage, proceed as in Exercise Six. As your confidence grows, the amount of thrusting can be increased but, for the moment, always do one stop/start exercise before you attempt penetration and keep to the woman-on-top position. Now the man can thrust a little so it is getting pretty close to a normal sexual encounter.

I like a couple to concentrate on this stage for quite some time and, if they are attending my clinic, I send them off to practise for about six week before we continue.

Exercise Eight

This is the last exercise and it involves the man being on top at the penetration stage. This is by far the most arousing moment for the premature ejaculator and, therefore, has to be approached with caution. Remember all the steps that you practised in masturbation and bring those into play now. So if you feel that you are getting close to coming, change position, slow down, take a break or do a Kegels. There are lots of options open to you and you don't have to rush to the finishing post. Pretty good feeling, don't you agree?

Delayed ejaculation

Another ejaculatory problem is that of delayed, or retarded, ejaculation, which does not present itself very often and is far more difficult to treat. This is a condition whereby the man cannot come at all or has great difficulty in coming. In some cases, he can come in masturbation but cannot come in the vagina, and in other cases, he cannot come at all in a female's presence. Of course, the premature ejaculator would give any-thing to be like the delayed ejaculator, but these men are usually most unhappy with their performance – or lack of it. Their partners tell a similar story. I remember one client telling me that she used to end up counting the number of thrusts and, when she got to 365, usually switched in her head to a list of things to do. Even more problematic is when such a couple are anxious for a baby. I have had some successes and some failures with delayed ejaculation, nevertheless, I would strongly rec-ommend somebody with this condition to seek the help of a qualified sex therapist. There can be a number of psychological reasons that are contributing to the condition, which the ther-apist can help unravel. It is also worthwhile consulting an urologist who in some cases can be of help.

I remember Michael and his wife, who came to see me at the clinic. Michael's absence of ejaculation was mainly due to his having been abused as a young altar boy and to the whole sense of shame that surrounded the abuse for him.

I worked also with a couple who came to see me having been to another counsellor for quite lengthy work on the man's inappropriate sexual relationship with his sister when his sister and he had both been much younger. He and his wife had completed the work with the other counsellor, who then referred them on to me for specific behavioural work on delayed ejaculation. In this case the programme suited the man very well and he was able to ejaculate within a reasonable length of time by the time they had completed therapy.

In the case of delayed ejaculation, the core of the problem is the man's inability to let go and the reasons why this is so need to be understood before anything can be done. For that reason I am not going to give a self-help programme of exercises for this condition. Seek professional help – you owe it to yourself and your partner.

[5]

COMMON DIFFICULTIES FOR WOMEN

Vaginismus

Vaginismus is a condition whereby the muscles at the entrance to the vagina contract and go into spasm. In most cases, the woman can allow nothing in past those muscles – not a finger, not a tampon, not a doctor to examine her and certainly not a penis. It is the condition I see most often in the clinic and the one that causes the most trauma to female clients. These women tell me that they feel quite different to everybody else; that they cringe when people make sexual jokes and innuendos; that, if they are married, are frequently asked when they are going to have a family; and that, when looking around a pub or a restaurant, they think everybody else in the building is having sex and they are not able to have it. They often think that they are the only ones that suffer from this and, since they have never talked to anybody else about it, other than a partner if they have one, they feel quite isolated.

Some women are able to allow a finger to enter the vagina, and others are able to use tampons, but none are able to allow penetration by a penis. They eventually seek help (and it can sometimes be years after they first experience the problem) for one of two reasons. Often they wish to become pregnant and know that the most direct way to become pregnant is by sexual intercourse. Secondly, they are afraid that their partner will leave them and go elsewhere for sex. Or, if they are single and have experienced vaginismus in a past relationship, they are afraid that it will deter future partners and so they want to do something about it. It takes a great deal of courage to admit to a complete stranger – which I am on that first meeting – that they have never had sexual intercourse, despite being with their current partner for, in some cases, fifteen years.

As regards the partners of these vaginismic women, they almost always fit into what I term a vaginismic partner profile. They are invariably really nice, laid-back guys, placid, with a very good sense of humour and they will always say to the woman that she is not to worry, that they will get there in the end. In other words, not at all pushy, whereas what she needs is somebody who *will* push, so this creates its own problem. Over the years, I have had the pleasure of working with so many of these men and have always looked forward to their visits and have been almost sad when treatment has ended. The amount of support they have given to their partners has been enormous and cannot be underestimated. As a consequence my life has been made much easier. Obviously, if I am working with a single woman, we cannot go as far as if she had a partner, but there is a great deal of work that can be done in order to prepare her for when she does want to have intercourse. I remember working with Margaret, who, when her treatment was finished, told me she was going to go off and have intercourse with somebody suitable. All she wanted to do was to get penetrative sex out of the way so that she would no longer be a virgin. She felt her sexual inexperience was like a great noose around her neck. About a week later I got a scribbled note, "The deed is done!!!"

So what is it that causes some women to be vaginismic? As always with dysfunctions, I break it down into *predisposing*, *precipitating* and *maintaining* factors.

PREDISPOSING FACTORS

This relates to how you were programmed by your parents in your childhood and what factors came into play as regards shaping your personality. These include your attitude to others, your relationship to your parents (particularly to your mother) your parents' relationship with each other, the attitudes towards sex in your home, the religious influences that you have encountered, sex education, your relationship to your siblings and all the things that went into your early formation.

Vaginismic women will often have come from a home where sex was not often spoken about – the television was turned off if anything sexual came on – so that they formed the impression early on that sex was something to be ashamed of and hushed up. They will usually have a very close bond with their parents, but particularly their mother. Sometimes it is *too* close in that they may still be living at home, although in their thirties, or will be in daily telephone contact with their mother and consult her at every turn. I remember one husband gently suggesting that it would be nice some nights to go straight home from work and eat at home rather than calling into his mother-in-law's house every evening and often staying for dinner.

It fits very well, then, that the last step in becoming an adult is cutting loose from home and being fully sexual, and some women are just not ready to do it – and their partner, if they fit the typical pattern, certainly isn't going to push them.

It was fascinating for me to observe Colleen work through a treatment programme. She was a twenty-one-year-old woman, just finishing college, whose mother had sent her to see me. She had vaginismus and had told her mother of the difficulties she was experiencing. Her mother not only found out where to send her daughter, but was paying for the treatment as well. During the history-taking interview, I ascertained that Colleen was, indeed, incredibly close to her mother and thought that her mother could do no wrong. I always point out to my clients my view that some relationships between parents and children can be so close as to be unhealthy and, after that, leave it up to themselves as to what they will do about it.

As Colleen progressed through treatment, she made various references to her mother but gradually some unflattering things were said and Colleen admitted that her mother seemed to have some faults after all. Then one day she said she would not be attending as frequently as before because she was now paying for the sessions herself. When we finally got to the end of treatment, by which time Colleen was having successful intercourse with her boyfriend (of whom mother did not approve), I asked if she was going to tell her mother the outcome. I was told that she certainly was not, that her sexual life had nothing to do with her mother. I heartily agreed.

PRECIPITATING FACTORS

These are actual events that have happened in your life that could have a bearing on the vaginismus. People sometimes underestimate the effect that an actual event, one that they consider quite insignificant, may have had on them. Or they may not connect the event with the problem. Some women think that, unless they have had abuse in their background, there can be no reason for the vaginismus. However, all sorts of things can contribute to it.

One woman told me how, when she was very young, her brother was reading a book he wasn't supposed to be reading and he kept it under his mattress. One day when he was out, she looked at the book and in it there was a very vivid description of a rape. She knew, even as she read it, that she would never be able to allow a man to penetrate her. Years later she was in my clinic with her boyfriend seeking help for long-standing vaginismus.

Another woman told me how her brother used to show her pornographic pictures just to watch her reaction and that was enough to make her scared of intercourse.

A client I worked with last year had never made the connection between the rough insertion of a catheter by a nurse, without warning, and her vaginismus until I pointed it out to her. She had been seven at the time and had a kidney infection. Indeed, she had many subsequent kidney infections all associated with pain in the genital area.

I could go on and on with examples of precipitating factors because each new vaginismic client brings a new one, but what I want to make clear is, that if you are suffering with vaginismus, do not underestimate any thing that may have contributed to the condition.

MAINTAINING FACTORS

These are the factors that keep the problem going. One of the key maintaining factors is the fact that most vaginismic women are worriers and they continue to worry right through treatment. So they achieve one step and immediately begin to worry about the next one. A worrier is inclined to be tense and, of course, this is mirrored in their vaginal muscles, which become so tense that they are unable to allow penetration. Often a maintaining factor is fear of pregnancy and, in my opinion, that alone has been great enough on occasions to cause the condition. The woman gets used to being unable to allow intercourse and, even if the situation has changed and it would now be all right for her to become pregnant, she cannot relax sufficiently to allow penetration.

Another maintaining factor is fear of pain, and the pain that these women experience is a very real pain, albeit produced by their minds. They will describe absolute searing pain when trying to have intercourse – it was explained to me once as being like putting hot curry paste on an open wound – and nobody is going to want to experience that too often.

Women with vaginismus are usually extremely sexual and fully enjoy the sexual experience, apart, of course, from the painful attempted intercourse. They evolve their own way of operating that allows them to be orgasmic and satisfy their partner very well. Often, they more than compensate for their inability to allow penetration by giving and receiving lots of satisfying oral sex and, generally, having a good time. So there is actually very little incentive for them to change, which is another maintaining factor.

Sometimes vaginismic women are penile phobic and cannot bear to look at or touch the penis. If that is the case, then obviously a lot of work needs to be done to get her to regard the penis as user-friendly before there can be any progress.

Some time ago I worked with Margaret and her husband Simon. They had three children without ever having had intercourse. His semen had been deposited near the entrance to the vagina and obviously his sperm were pretty good swimmers! She had her third baby by the natural childbirth method because she felt that, if she went through all that, then she would surely be able to allow a penis in. She progressed very quickly through the treatment programme, but ground to a firm halt when we got to the point where the penis was beginning to be inserted. I was fairly stuck myself with her treatment, but decided to spend some time on actually discussing the penis with her and her thoughts about it. I asked her when she had first seen an erect penis, as that can often cause problems if it has been traumatic. "I never saw one", was her reply and I found out that she was totally penile phobic. When we had spent some time working on that aspect, she felt much freer and was able to go ahead and have intercourse.

Treatment

So what do you do if you have vaginismus? This is one condition that I believe benefits enormously from working with a psycho-sexual therapist, as very often the woman needs the constant encouragement and reassurance that a therapist can give. As I have explained, a lot of the time the problems are in a woman's head, and to emphasise this I would like you to read the following extract which was sent to me by a former client. Read it right to the end.

GIRL'S FIRST TIME

Assume you are a girl (if you are a guy). It's your first time. As you lie back your muscles tighten. You put him off for a while searching for an excuse, but he refuses to be swayed as he approaches you. He asks if you are afraid and you shake your head bravely. He has had more experience, but it is the first time his finger has found the right place. He probes deeply and you shiver; your body tenses but he is gentle like he promised you he would be. He looks deeply into your eyes and tells you to trust him – he has done this many times before. His cool smile relaxes you and you open wider to give him more room for an easy entrance. You begin to plead and beg him to hurry, but he slowly takes his time, wanting to cause you as little pain as possible. As he presses closer, going deeper, you feel the tissue give way; pain surges throughout your body and you feel the slight trickle of blood as he continues. He looks at you concerned and asks you if it is too painful. Your eyes are filled with tears but you shake your head and nod for him to go on. He begins going in and out with skill but you are now too numb to feel him within you. After a few moments, you feel something bursting within you and he pulls it out of you. You lie panting, glad to have it over. He looks at you and, smiling warmly, tells you with a chuckle that you have been his most stubborn yet most rewarding experience. You smile and thank your dentist. After all, it was your first time to have a tooth pulled.

Now what were you thinking as you read that? See how active the imagination can be?

However, if the option of therapy is not open to you for whatever reason then certainly you can do quite a lot of work to help things along either on your own, or with a partner. Actually the majority of work will probably be done on your own so don't worry too much if you do not have a partner (and remember that vaginismic women are terrible worriers).

Firstly, try to identify for yourself why it is you have vaginismus. It will help you if you can understand, even a little, your predisposing, precipitating and maintaining factors. If one of the factors is any form of abuse in your background then, firstly, you should get professional help dealing specifically with the abuse.

Exercises

PREPARING THE ROOM
Make sure that the room that you are using (probably the bedroom) is nice and warm, as you will be lying on the bed wearing only a robe and if you feel even a little chilly this will be counterproductive. Light a few candles – you can use some lovely scented ones – or have subdued lighting, as you are trying to create a little haven for yourself. Have some music going in the background, tapes or CDs are best as the radio always has presenters and they can be distracting. Lastly, do a quick tidy up to add to the general feeling of calm rather than chaos.

PREPARING YOURSELF
Have a relaxing bath or shower. Generally the bath is more relaxing, but if that is not possible then a shower is fine. Use whatever your favourite bath preparation is, whether it be bubbles, gel or bath oil and simply relax. I had one client who lit a whole lot of candles around the bath and adored that time for herself.

While you are in the bath, begin to take notice of what the water feels like on your skin and what sensation the bubbles produce, and generally get used to focusing on the sensations in your body. Then take your time drying yourself – use a nice fluffy towel – and again focus on the sensations. You are now ready to begin the exercises. I would suggest that you do each exercise a minimum of three times on three different occasions preferably a day or two apart and do not move onto the next one until you are perfectly comfortable with the current one. Finally, don't forget that as soon as one exercise is done you will start worrying about the next. This is normal!

EXERCISES FOR YOU ONLY

You need to allocate some time to working on your vaginismus. I recommend that you set aside three different periods of forty-five minutes each week. Choose a time when you are not going to be too tired (therefore, not too late at night), when you can guarantee that you will not be disturbed and when you can take the phone off the hook, ensure that somebody else will answer it or put an answering machine on. This is going to be your time for *yourself* and it is most important that you are relaxed both mentally and physically.

Exercise One

Stand in front of a full-length mirror and look at your naked body front and back. This is often difficult as we are never fully happy with our bodies. The only change we can make to ourselves, short of surgery, is to either lose or gain weight. The latter seems to be very easy for most of us who see ourselves as being too fat anyway. However, people who feel themselves to be too thin tell me that it is almost impossible to put on weight. What I am saying is that, if we cannot alter the shape or our stomach/breasts/legs/neck or whatever it is we are unhappy with, then we have to be able to accept ourselves as we are. So instead of focusing on all the negative things, find three things about your body that you really like and focus on them for a change. It can be your ears, your toes, legs, bottom or anything else. Just find these three things and be happy. Having done this, go to your bed. This is a preliminary exercise to get you used to looking at your own body and when you are comfortable with this you can skip this step and go straight to the bed.

Now I want you to experiment with touching your body while applying body lotion or oil. Make sure that the lotion is at body temperature – having it in the bath or shower with you will ensure this – and slowly and gently apply the lotion to all accessible parts of your body. Try rubbing it in gently, then briskly, strongly and then very lightly so you can see how you actually like to be touched and stroked. Take your time doing this and when you have covered as much of your body as possible take a few minutes to just lie there and reflect on your thoughts about your body. Repeat this exercise on three separate occasions.

Exercise Two

Having completed Exercise One again, I now want you to continue by concentrating on looking at the genital area. Generally, this is an area about which women are fairly ignorant and an awful lot of women have never actually looked at it at all. Now how are you going to feel comfortable allowing somebody else to look, touch and put an erect penis in if you don't have a clue, yourself, about what it is like to look at and touch? So start by looking. Unfortunately, we cannot look at what is there without using a mirror and both hands – as with everything else, women are far more complicated than men. Get a small mirror and prop it up against a pillow. Then put another pillow behind your back and spread your legs. (See *Figure 6* on *page 36*.)

Use both hands to pull apart your outer lips to reveal the inner lips, then locate the various bits that comprise the vulval area. There is the vaginal opening, which may or may not have an intact hymen. Chances are that your hymen is already broken as this can happen in all sorts of ways, either through sport or through using tampons if you have been able to do so. Many women think that an unbroken hymen is at the root of all their problems, but it's probably not the case. I have rarely seen women with hymen so rigid that surgery was required to break it; it is usually a simple matter for it to be broken. Think more of the hymen as being just a membrane and you will have a better idea of what is involved. Above the vaginal opening is the urethra through which the urine flows and this is a very, very small opening. Above the urethra is the nerve centre of a woman – that is, the clitoris.

If this is your first time looking at your genital area, you will probably get a shock – it is never quite what we expected, and usually a lot redder than we thought it was going to be. I often equate it with looking inside our mouths (but without the teeth).

Now you have looked once, the next time is not going to be quite so frightening, and remember that no two genital areas look the same – just like faces – so do not be worried if you think yours is quite different to any photographs you may have seen. It certainly will not look like *Figure 6*, but this diagram will help in locating the various bits.

Exercise Three

You have now looked and become acquainted, or reacquainted, with your genital area. When you are quite comfortable with this it is time to begin touching. Some women have a lot of difficulty with touching this area, so do not worry if it takes you some time to be comfortable doing so. In fact, some people begin by using surgical gloves and after some time (which can be minutes in some cases, weeks or months in others) are able to move on to using their fingers without a glove. Others begin by using a cotton bud – whatever it is that helps you move forward is fine. I would suggest that from now on when you are doing your exercises that you use some form of lubricant. KY Jelly, Senselle or any of the brands that you can pick up in your local pharmacy will help you, as they replicate very well the natural lubrication that takes place in the vagina when the woman is aroused and therefore ease insertion. You are not inserting anything for the moment, just getting comfortable with touching this area that up until now has had very negative associations for you, but it helps to start using the lubricant and having positive associations about that.

Exercise Four

This exercise is one that you will use constantly from now on. Its called Kegels exercise because it was a Dr Kegels who discovered the muscles that you will be using and they are the muscles that you actually contract when you are unable to allow anything into the vagina. To locate these muscles, imagine you are giving a mid-stream urine sample, that is, that you are urinating and then stopping in mid-flow. The muscles that you use to stop the flow are the muscles I want you to use in this exercise.

Now picture in your mind that these muscles are actually the doors of an elevator and you are the elevator operator. Starting on the ground floor with the doors closed you open the muscles to open the doors. People get in and you then close the doors. Up to the first floor and you open the doors again. Some people get out and then more get in, so keep the doors open. Everybody in, close the doors and onto the second floor. The same thing happens here, so repeat the process and then up to the third floor. This time people get out and nobody gets in, so you close the doors and go all the way back down to the ground floor and open the doors again. As you are reading this, of course, your muscles are open and you are nice and relaxed, but whenever you get anxious about your genital area your natural instinct is to close those muscles tight. What you are doing in this exercise is taking control of those muscles so that *you* decide when they will open or close. This is a great exercise and you will need to do it a number of times a day, whenever you think of it. After all, nobody else knows you are doing it!

Exercise Five

You are now ready to start with inserting one finger in the vagina. Of course, you will be apprehensive about this, but if you have done all the previous steps then it really is a natural progression. There is no need to look in a mirror while doing this, just feel your way and try to relax. If you feel it is very daunting then do some deep breathing or some relaxation exercises to begin with. Adopt the same position as when you are looking at your genital area, put some lubricant on your third finger, rub the finger up and down the inner lips and, when you locate the vaginal opening, do three Kegels exercises slowly. When you are sure the muscles are in the open position then start to insert the finger slowly. Be aware that the finger does not go straight in but rather curves upwards.

Take it gently and, if you are relaxed enough, your finger will go in. You may meet some initial resistance but persevere and you will get there. Some women feel sure that they are feeling some bone and that they cannot get past that, but believe me there is an opening there and it is ready for you to explore. Remember that there are very few nerve endings in the vagina so there is very little to fear. It may take a few attempts to get the finger in, and that is normal. The more often you do it, the easier it becomes and, finally, you feel comfortable with it and delighted with yourself that you have achieved it. Well done! Repeat this exercise in two subsequent sessions until you feel confident to move on.

Exercise Six

This is an extension of Exercise Five in that you now use two fingers instead of one, the middle and index with the middle on top of the index. It is a bit more awkward to manage, but it gets you used to a slightly thicker circumference going in and it is, therefore, well worth doing. As usual, you should do this exercise successfully three times before moving on.

Exercise Seven

You should wait until you have a period before proceeding to Exercise Seven, as you are now ready to move on to tampon insertion. To have the option of using tampons instead of towels is a boon to most women. Some of my clients tell me that, when they get to be able to use them, they will often carry a tampon around in their bags even when they are not menstruating because they feel they are now one of the gang. I remember Eithne who was so excited at getting a tampon inserted that she telephoned her husband on his mobile and started shouting, "I got a tampon in, isn't that great news!" At that moment, he was paying a cab driver in Belfast who heard the conversation much to her husband's embarrassment.

When your next period arrives, have a box of tampons ready. Use the ones that have an applicator and start off with the slim size. Be well acquainted with the instructions and take one or two apart so that you are not frightened of them. Run some water on the tampon when it is out of the applicator and see how soft it becomes. When it comes to inserting one, follow the instructions that come with the pack. Most women find that they are easiest to apply with one foot up on the toilet bowl. Use your Kegels exercises before you attempt insertion, take your time, relax and remember that you already have had success with one and two fingers. Gradually your brain is taking in the concept that things can go in and out of your vagina without pain. And remember the tampon goes in the same direction as the fingers, back at an angle rather than straight back.

You have now completed a whole section of exercises and are well on the way to curing your vaginismus. In some cases, women can already insert fingers and tampons and also allow a partner's fingers to be inserted and, if that is the case, you can continue on from here, but be sure to begin each session with a bath or shower as I described earlier.

Exercise Eight

Some years ago a wonderful product came on the market for women suffering with vaginismus. It comprises a series of vaginal trainers called Amielle Trainers and, in my experience with clients, they have been of great assistance. They are manufactured by Owen Mumford Ltd, Brook Hill, Woodstock, Oxfordshire, OX20 1TU, England (telephone: (+44)1993 812021, fax: (+44)1993 813466) and you can contact them to either obtain a set or to find the name of a local supplier.

The trainers come in four graded sizes (No. 1 is the smallest) and are conical shaped. When you first see them please do not start worrying about the larger ones. I actually give them to clients one by one over a period of time, as I know from experience vaginismic women will worry unduly. The first one is a bit larger than a tampon, so it is very logical to go on to No.1 when you have been successful with tampon insertion.

These trainers are supplied with a handle, which some women like to use and others do not. As with the previous exercises using your fingers, have a bath, relax, lie on your back with your legs apart, do three Kegels exercises slowly, apply a lubricant to trainer No. 1 and begin to insert it. You will probably find that it goes in relatively easily, as you are so well prepared. When you are used to inserting it while lying on your back, adopt a position as if you were on top in love-making and insert it, again slowly. You will probably feel very silly doing this but the reason is that when you first attempt intercourse it will be with you on top. This is because it is very important for a vaginismic woman to feel in control, as she does in this position, so you should get used to it in advance.

Exercise Nine

On now to trainer No. 2, but I always suggest to clients that they use No. 1 just prior to using No.2 to remind themselves to keep the muscles open and also to prepare the vagina. When you feel comfortable with trainer No. 2 you are already half way through the series of trainers so you should feel very pleased with yourself.

Exercise Ten

No. 3 trainer often causes a lot of concern when it is produced. This is because it is getting to be like the real thing in size and the woman immediately gets tense because, previously, she simply was not able to allow a penis in and now here is some-thing that is very similar. So it is a big step to take. To reassure yourself, go back and look at No. 2 and you will see that it fits into No.3 and so it is really only one size up. It is also very important to realise that, to quote Zilbergeld, author of *The New Male Sexuality* (Bantam, New York, 1999), the vagina is "a potential and not a space" and it can stretch to accommodate whatever is asked of it, whether it is a finger or a baby's head, and it will always hug whatever is in there. Your vagina can stretch perfectly to accommodate this trainer, but to enable this to happen you need to relax those muscles, accept a little discomfort and push on.

Do not expect that you will be successful with No. 3 the first time you try it, be patient and if you can take it in even past the muscles at the opening to the vagina then that is wonderful. Next time you will be able to go a little further, and so on. Don't give up. It sometimes takes a lot of trying before there is success. Just believe in yourself and believe that you *can* do it.

I find it helps if the woman gets herself aroused, through masturbation, to a degree where she is producing her own lubrication and her body has started the internal changes that I explain in *Chapter 3* but this is not absolutely necessary. It also can help if she places a pillow under her bottom as this slightly alters the angle and makes it easier for her to insert the trainer. Some of my clients have had great success with this exercise in the bath, so experiment with whatever works for you. When you have been successful with No. 3, while lying on your back, repeat the process in the woman-on-top position as you did with the previous trainers.

Exercise Eleven

Here you are ready to use the very last trainer, and this is, in fact, optional. What I suggest is that, for a woman without a partner, it is great to have the confidence of having worked through No. 4, but often a woman who has a partner will decide that her man has a penis that is closer in size to No. 3

than to No. 4. The choice is up to you, and all the same instructions for No. 3 hold good for No.4.

For a woman without a partner this is obviously as far as you can go but you should be very confident and hopeful that any future attempt at sexual intercourse will prove to be successful. Sometimes my single clients go on to use a vibrator which can be both satisfying for them and good practise. Again, the choice is yours.

EXERCISES WITH A PARTNER

For those of you with a partner, it will be necessary for you to go through all the steps for working on your own but, in conjunction with that, you should also be doing the following exercises with your partner.

You should always be one step ahead with your work on your own, so that anything you attempt with your partner you have already done yourself. This helps to build your confidence, reduce your anxiety and, therefore, helps you to relax.

First of all plan your sessions. It sounds a bit clinical, and indeed is a bit clinical, but that way you ensure that you have regular sessions, that you make progress and that no hidden agendas creep in. Aim to have at least two sessions a week and if you can manage three that would be great.

> *From now until you are told otherwise, there is a ban on attempted intercourse, orgasm and ejaculation. There is no ban on masturbation to climax, but not in each other's presence.*

> *Every session should be preceded by a bath or shower. While one person showers, the other should prepare the room. Make sure it is warm, have subdued lighting, maybe light a few candles and put on some background music – answerphones should be turned on for all phones.*

Exercise One

You will use this hour to give and receive massage. Divide the hour into two halves and give each other a massage devoting roughly fifteen minutes to each side of the body. However, for the moment skip the breasts, the genital area and the buttocks. The purpose of the massage is to see how you like to touch your partner and to be touched by him, but in a non-sexual way, although you are both naked. This is called sensate focus because you are using all of the senses: seeing, hearing, taste, touch and smell. The sense of taste is covered by giving little butterfly kisses, whenever you feel like it, to whatever parts of the body takes your fancy, except for the areas mentioned above. Vary the touch you are using to see what you like most.

Start by getting your partner to lie on their stomach with their arms stretched above their head. Begin at the head and, taking your time, experience all the different contours of their head and hair using different strokes. Move on slowly down the back, up along the arms and massage the individual fingers. Cover the entire body in this way right down to the toes but skip the buttocks. Then get them to turn over on their back and you begin again starting with the face. Don't forget the kisses. If you are a man, do not touch your partner's breasts or genital area; if you are a woman, skip the genital area.

We all feel more vulnerable when lying on our back, so be sensitive to this with your partner. After all our whole body is fully exposed with all the lumps, bumps, scar marks and the bits we may be unhappy about in full view! I ask people to do this exercise initially with just their bare hands and then to add whatever lotion or oil they like so that they can experience the difference.

Sometimes a woman is unable to allow her full body to be exposed and so it is all right to use something like a scarf to cover the areas she has a problem with – usually the breasts, genital area and/or bottom – until she has got used to the whole idea of relaxing with her partner, then gradually remove the scarf.

At the end of each session spend a few minutes in each other's arms talking and having a cuddle and telling each other what the time was like for you. It is after all a very intimate exercise. You can have sex with a perfect stranger, but there is no way that you would give that same stranger the intimate massage you have just shared with your partner. Complete this exercise a further two times.

Exercise Two

As with earlier exercises, do not move on to this one until you have done the previous one successfully three times. Now you are ready to move on to including the breasts and the genital area in the massage. Remember that touching these areas is part of an overall massage so do not go for those areas with a view to helping arousal, as sometimes this can happen far too quickly for the woman's liking. In this exercise, the man should only brush his fingers over the pubic hair as he massages his partner and when the woman is massaging him she should touch his penis in a way that she is comfortable with. In some cases she may never really have touched it before and therefore this will be quite a big step for her.

Exercise Three

Repeat the mutual massage, as outlined in Exercise One, to start the session and then proceed as follows.

As the woman will already have done this exercise herself, she should now be comfortable enough to allow her partner to explore her genital area in some detail, which will involve him opening the outer lips and exposing the inner lips. Again, this is done in the context of beginning at the top of the body and working down. The woman should spend some more time touching and becoming friendly with her partner's penis (I have yet to have a man object to this) and get used to the feel of it. She will find it is not the horrible thing that she was terrified of, but just a piece of spongy tissue that, when erect, feels warm and silky to the touch. It may become inadvertently erect when the woman touches it so use the opportunity to explore! Start telling each other where and how you like to be touched so that there is positive feedback between you.

Exercise Four

By now you should both be happy to give and receive massage and to be relaxed with each other's bodies. So now you move on to arousal. You still want to keep the session within the hour, so reduce the actual massage to twenty minutes for each person, ten minutes each side. The difference is that now you are going to be aware that you will be working towards arousal so, at the end of the massage, you continue on with mutual touching, kissing and doing whatever it is that you know helps to get your partner aroused.

You then should move into what I call the trust position, where the woman lies with her head against his shoulder, both facing the same way forward as if in a rowing boat. She will then be able to allow him to insert his third finger in her vagina, presuming, of course, that she has become sufficiently aroused and that she has done a Kegels exercise to ensure she is ready. For his part, he should be sure that his fingernail is trimmed with no jagged edges and he must be ready to stop at any times that she asks him to. The reward for all of this is that the ban on orgasm and ejaculation is removed – things are looking up – and you can then go on to reach a climax whatever way you wish.

Figure 8:
Man stimulating
woman.

Exercise Five

Proceed as instructed in Exercise Four but, in this exercise, the man uses two fingers. It can be helpful for him to use a lubricant on his fingers, as this is what his partner has become used to in her own work.

Depending on where the woman has got to in her own programme, the couple may need to take a pause in their joint work at this point. This is because I have found that, in the long run, it is more beneficial if the woman has finished work with trainer No. 3, or indeed trainer No. 4, if the size of his erect penis is still an issue for her.

Exercise Six

This exercise is a lovely bridge between the trainers and the penis. The couple should no longer use the man's fingers. Instead they should get used to the woman being on top and playing with the penis up and down the labia. This adds to the woman's enjoyment and gets her used to holding the penis in preparation for inserting it.

Exercise Seven

This exercise also involves the woman on top but, in this exercise, she progresses to holding the erect penis and using it to 'plug' the entrance to the vagina. This is so she can get used to the feel of an erect penis at the entrance to the vagina.

I notice that I have begun to use the words 'erect penis' a lot at this point and I should just add that this can sometimes be a problem for men. Here is the poor guy, who all this time has been told he cannot have intercourse, and now he is expected to produce erections on demand. Sometimes stage fright ensues and the guys come in to me rather shamefacedly saying that I will never guess what happened. I usually guess straightaway, as it is so understandable. In these instances, inevitably, the woman is almost pleased that for once it is not *she* that has the problem and that he now has some idea as to how she felt for all this time! If no erection happens, please don't worry. It is perfectly natural and will right itself very soon.

Exercise Eight

Finally the end is in sight! Go through the routine that you have been practising, with the woman on top holding the penis to guide it into the vagina, until you are both aroused. She will need to push herself down on it because it is not going to go in of its own accord – the man must *not* move at this stage. It is very hard to say to a couple exactly what to do at this point as for some couples the penis goes in almost all the way and for others the woman is only comfortable in taking in a piece at a time.

Be aware that, for *any* couple having intercourse, it takes a couple of movements for the penis to fit snugly into the vagina. So you are no different from any other couple if this happens in your case. At the beginning, it is important that the movement should only come from the woman as she has to feel totally in control – hence her being on top. Only when she feels all right with having the penis inside, or partially inside, should she allow the man to move. Gradually you will become familiar with this new experience (often for both of you) and gradually grow to like it and actually have fun.

If you suffer from vaginismus, I know it is hard for you to believe that you can actually have intercourse successfully. But the difference between somebody suffering with vaginismus and me (or another sex therapist) is that I have actually seen an awful lot of women go through treatment successfully, whereas *you* probably do not know one other single person who has it. Therefore, you have to take my word for it. But believe me, when it is all over and you are six months down the road, you will truly wonder what all the fuss was about and why you were unable to do this all along.

Ted and Eileen were, a couple I worked with some years ago. Eileen had ended her relationship with Ted when she first came to see me because she did not think it was fair to be depriving him of the experience of sexual intercourse since he was also a virgin. After a few months, however, she told me that Ted was back on the scene because he had been so lonely without her that he insisted she take him back. We worked on

99

her vaginismus for a really long time – I remember Ted sat three different driving tests during this treatment. He had a great sense of humour and told me that when they were just about to have penetration for the first time he stopped her and said, "What if, after all this time, I don't like it?" Fortunately, he did like it and, hopefully, they are still having a good time together.

Another couple, who had been married for two years but had no sexual intercourse, due to her having been abused by a brother, were finally successful. However that, too, presented difficulties. A few days after their first successful intercourse, he came to see me and told me he didn't know if he would be able for it all. Apparently, their first session had gone on for a really long time and a few hours later they had another go, just to be sure it still worked. He was fairly unfit and, the next morning, had to drag himself into work absolutely exhausted. I reassured him that the novelty would soon pass.

Enjoy every moment of practising your newfound skills.

[6]

ORGASMIC DIFFICULTIES FOR WOMEN

There is a great line in one of Bette Midler's mono-
logues. Bette plays a character called Soph who says,
"My boyfriend often asks me why I never tell him
when I'm having an orgasm. So I tell him it's because he is
never around!" And for a lot of women it is easier to orgasm
through masturbation than through intercourse. The reason
for this is twofold. Firstly, around 70 per cent of women do
not orgasm through intercourse *alone*, as they need extra stimulation of the clitoris. Secondly, orgasm is all about letting
go and some women find it extremely difficult to let go in
front of a man. Indeed, in some cases they just find it difficult
to let go – even on their own – and that is why, if you are
experiencing difficulties regarding orgasm, you should practise
on your own first. For once and for all let us get rid of the idea
that the guy is responsible for the woman's orgasm – he is not.
He may be a large contributor to it, either by his physical
presence or in her fantasy, but a woman is ultimately responsible
for her own orgasm.

I remember Jim coming to see me because his girlfriend was
not having an orgasm with him and he wondered what he was
doing wrong. I thought it was wonderful that he cared that much
to come and see me, but I felt strongly, as I tried to reassure

him that he was doing nothing wrong at all, that it was the *girlfriend* who should have been sitting opposite me rather than Jim.

Historically, there appears to have been much more emphasis on male ejaculation than on female orgasm and presumably nature has had something to do with this. After all, it is possible for a woman to become pregnant without her having an orgasm but impossible for pregnancy to occur, in the normal way, without the man ejaculating. However, now that women have more of a voice than they used to have and are equal partners in the sexual area, they are much more forthcoming about their needs. And indeed they *do* deserve to have an orgasm when making love every bit as much as their male counterparts.

As I see it, one of the problems a couple encounters is that the woman usually takes a lot longer than the man to become aroused to the point of orgasm and by then he may well have come, leaving her high and wet! At this point she needs to be a bit assertive in letting him know that she is not there yet. Hopefully he is a considerate lover and, even though he has already come, will help her along to reach climax too. Or if he can delay his own orgasm, so much the better. A lot of women tell me that they feel a bit selfish asking for this and are afraid that their man will get tired of stimulating them, but most men will actually be delighted to do so as it is a very satisfying feeling to have contributed to a partner's orgasm.

As I've said before, just think of the man and woman as being equivalent to gas and electricity. *He* is the gas and *she* is the electricity. It takes the gas a far shorter time to bring a pot to the boil and, as soon as it is turned off, the pot grows cold very quickly. Electricity, on the other hand, takes much longer to bring a pot to boiling point, but it can keep the pot simmering for quite a while even after it is has been turned off. Similarly, a woman can keep simmering, having more orgasms like little after-waves, whereas the man has only one ejaculation and loses the erection shortly afterwards. The important thing to remember is that both gas and electricity can perform the same function!

Couples that have been together for some time usually evolve a way of making love that suits them both. Some couples have the woman come first, then the man. Others, especially if he comes fairly quickly, will have him come first and then, after some time, his partner.

The woman may reach orgasm during intercourse or, in many cases, outside intercourse. If it is to happen during intercourse, she will often need extra stimulation to bring her to a climax. This is because the indirect stimulation of the clitoris, provided by the penis moving in and out of the vagina and tugging on the vaginal lips (which are attached to the clitoris), is often not enough. So one or other of them may have to use their fingers to stimulate the clitoris as well. Or to provide variety, they may use a vibrator from time to time. Or she may rub on his pubic bone while lying on top of him. The possibilities are endless and there is no right way, only what is right for you.

Couples also experiment with positions. Obviously, as regards female orgasm, more of her body is available to be stimulated if she is on top and he has his hands free. However, some women don't like this position, especially if they are unhappy with their figures for whatever reason, as there is more possibility of the wobbly bits wobbling! So, for them, perhaps one of the side-by-side positions, where the couple face each other, is better. This position can produce quite intense feelings of heightened arousal and, therefore, is more likely to lead to orgasm. The disadvantage of this position, however, is that, because the thrusting is quite shallow, the penis tends to slip out easily, which can upset the flow of things – hopefully producing some laughter! (See *Figure 9* on *page 104* and *pages 155* and *172* for alternative side-by-side positions.)

Figure 9
Side-by-side
position.

What is an orgasm?

So far I have been talking about those of you who have had the
experience of orgasm. What if you have never had one? What
does it feel like and how do you know if you have had one?
Well, an orgasm is a series of contractions felt in the genital
area that are extremely pleasurable and last for about ten to
fifteen seconds. For some women this can be a very strong
feeling, for others quite gentle. But all women share the same
feelings afterwards – a very relaxed state in which she does
not want to be touched in the genital area for a little while
and often will feel like having a little sleep. In fact, some
people masturbate in order to achieve the feelings of relaxation
that enable them to get to sleep at night and I have had
clients who have this goal in mind when they come to me – a
really good night's sleep. The orgasmic state is reached by the
woman becoming aroused and then stimulating the clitoris
fairly strongly while at the same time remaining turned-on
mentally.

Don't be misled by books or the movies – every orgasm is
not earth shattering and accompanied by violent shudders
and screams – that is often poetic licence on behalf of the

ORGASMIC DIFFICULTIES FOR WOMEN

filmmakers. One client of mine told me that she would stop herself having an orgasm whenever she got close to it, as she was afraid that she would lose all control and start making a whole load of noise and banging against the wall with her legs and then the neighbours would hear. She was an avid reader and was basing her knowledge on the Jackie Collins type of character. She was actually a little disappointed when she finally did have an orgasm and discovered that it was much less than she had anticipated, but at least she stopped worrying about the neighbours.

Not all women have an orgasm through clitoral stimulation. I have come across a few women who can reach orgasm just through clenching and unclenching the vaginal muscles quickly and one woman told me that it was so easy for her she often had one on the bus just to pass the time. However, these women are pretty unusual and orgasm is almost always reached through clitoral stimulation of some sort.

If you are having difficulties bringing yourself to orgasm or having an orgasm with a partner there are some exercises that will help you which I give below. But first you will need to discover what it is that is causing you to have this problem. Are you a person who needs to feel in control at all times? If so, you should start by looking at other areas in your life where you could begin to make some changes in order to loosen up a little. So, if you find that you are compulsively tidy or that you tend to control your partner, try altering this in some way. Maybe you could let your room be untidy for a change, or stop yourself being a back-seat driver and see how that feels for you. Loosening up in these ways really will help you get into a better frame of mind for letting go sexually too. As I said at the beginning of this chapter, the first step is to practise by yourself and then later with a partner if you have one. Remember, it is physically possible for *any* woman to have an orgasm, it is just a question of finding what works for you. For the time being we will concentrate on you alone.

FAKING AN ORGASM

A few thoughts on faking it. As anyone who has watched *When Harry Met Sally* (1989) will know, it is easy to fake an orgasm if you are a good actress. A lot of women will say to me that they occasionally fake it, and it's often because they have had enough, either through boredom or tiredness, and it's an easy way out. Their partner thinks that it was great for them, so *he* is happy and she gets to sleep, so *she* is happy. However, I have seen couples where she has been faking it on a regular basis and he has somehow found out and this has caused very real relationship difficulties. In some of these cases, the man has been incredibly hurt and has lost trust in his partner, as well as having his self-confidence pretty shaken. For this reason, I am very much against anything more than occasional faking.

FEMALE EJACULATION

I should mention that a small percentage of women experience ejaculation on orgasm. It is not urine, there is quite a large quantity and it can be very embarrassing if the man has not been previously warned. Indeed I had a couple, Anne and Vincent, who came to me because of Vincent's premature ejaculation. After they had been with me for quite some time, Anne told me that she rarely orgasmed because she always urinated at the same time. She had never heard of female ejaculation and was incredibly relieved when I told her that it was not in fact urine and was a known phenomenon.

Exercises

PREPARING THE ROOM

Make sure that the room that you are using (probably the bedroom) is nice and warm, as you will be lying on the bed wearing only a robe and if you feel even a little chilly this will be counterproductive. Light a few candles – you can use some lovely scented ones – or have subdued lighting as you are trying to create a little haven for yourself. Have some music going in the background, tapes or CDs are best as the radio always has presenters and they can be distracting. Lastly, do a quick tidy up to add to the general feeling or calm rather than chaos.

PREPARING YOURSELF
Have a relaxing bath or shower. Generally the bath is more relaxing, but if that is not possible then a shower is fine. Use whatever your favourite bath preparation is, whether it be bubbles, gel or bath oil and simply relax. I had one client who lit a whole lot of candles around the bath and adored that time for herself.

While you are in the bath begin to take notice of what the water feels like on your skin and what sensation the bubbles produce and generally get used to focusing on the sensations in your body. Then take your time drying yourself – use a nice fluffy towel – and again focus on the sensations. You are now ready to begin the exercises. I would suggest that you do each exercise a minimum of three times on three different occasions preferably a day or two apart and do not move on to the next one until you are perfectly comfortable with the current one.

EXERCISES FOR YOU ONLY
I recommend that you set aside two or, if at all possible, three different periods of forty-five minutes each week. Choose a time when you are not going to be too tired (therefore not too late at night), when you can guarantee that you will not be disturbed and when you can take the phone off the hook, ensure that somebody else will answer it or put an answering machine on. This is going to be your time for yourself and it is most important that you are relaxed both mentally and physically.

Exercise One

Allocate some time for yourself. Somehow this is often very difficult for women as they are always on the go and feel quite guilty about taking time out for themselves, although they are always there for everybody else. After your warm bath or shower, you should be feeling relaxed.

Lie on your bed and massage as much of your body as you comfortably can with some warm body lotion or oil, at the same time letting your mind drift away from the day-to-day things that are in it. Picture some scene from the past where you were perfectly happy and bring yourself back to that place. It may have been outdoors or indoors, winter or summer, alone or with somebody else. The main thing is that it was a time when you felt perfectly content. You may have to sift a little through your memory bank to recover the scene, but once you do you will be able to go there in your mind's eye very quickly. Think a little about that time – the smells, sounds, conversations, thoughts – and enjoy it. It will greatly help your relaxation.

When you have done at least ten minutes of massage allow your hand to go to your genital area and gently massage it also. Nothing specific, just experiment with general touching and see how it feels. You will probably notice a slightly warm feeling in that area which is vaguely pleasurable. That is enough for now and you have done very well if you have achieved all that I suggested.

Exercise Two

Begin by massaging your body with lotion for about ten minutes, including your breasts and any other area that you may find erogenous and move your body as you massage, then progress to some more touching of the vaginal area.

However, this time start to move gently and rhythmically, as if simulating intercourse. Start investigating your clitoral area, rubbing it gently with your third finger. Try circular movements and rubbing each side. The clitoris is a really sensitive area and it can get sore from very direct stimulation, so you need to figure out just how you like yours to be touched in order to pass this information on to your lover when the time comes. At this stage, use some lubricating jelly, as it can be very helpful in promoting your own lubrication, especially if you have a tendency to dryness. Continue this for a few minutes. You should do this exercise a few times over the course of a week.

Exercise Three

Again, begin by massaging your body with lotion for about ten minutes, including your breasts and any other area that you may find erogenous and move your body as you massage, then progress to some more touching of the vaginal area.

By now you should be experiencing some sort of pleasurable sexual sensations, so it is now time to move on to *thinking* more sexually and to fantasising. Fantasy is a word that scares a lot of people, because they feel they don't know how to do it. Yet, if I ask them what they would do if they won the lottery, they have no problem in telling me. So fantasising sexually is no more than that – just letting your imagination roam free to whatever sexual moment you would like to participate in, real or imagined. It can be something from your past or something you would really like to happen in the future or something that you would like to try out but know you never will in reality. It does not matter at all what your fantasy is, as long as it takes your mind away from the here and now and concentrates it on thinking sexually. If you find this difficult then there is lots of reading material available. Try one of the Nancy Friday books such as *My Secret Garden* (Hutchinson, London, 1979) or *Woman On Top* (Hutchinson, London, 1991) and, in flicking through them, you will find something that turns you on.

From now on you are, more or less, beginning to tease yourself. So when you get turned on by touching the breasts, move down to the genital area. If you like what you are doing to the clitoris, stop for a little while and move to the entrance of the vagina and insert a finger. Move the finger around a little and take it out again. Then try using the heel of your hand on the clitoris so that it is indirectly stimulated. Be guided by what your body feels it would like. Now begin to concentrate more and more on the clitoris making the stimulation quicker and quicker as most women need quite fast stimulation in order to bring them to climax. Continue this for as long as it feels good and repeat on two other occasions.

Exercise Four

By now you should be getting used to the nice feelings you are capable of producing and will want to get on to reaching a climax. Every person varies in what works for them but below are some suggestions that can help you reach the final destination.

- Clench and unclench your vaginal muscles really quickly to produce a fluttering sensation. These are the muscles that you clench when you need to urinate and have to hang on for a few minutes. This simulates what will actually happen in orgasm and is helpful for that reason.

- Breathe heavily and act out what you think will happen when you reach a climax as regards sounds or words.

- Change your position. Just as you move position in intercourse it is natural to move position in masturbation. Try different positions, lie on your side or on your tummy but keep up the stimulation at the same time.

- Use a vibrator. My clients have tried various vibrators over the years and they seem to prefer the more pliable type to the rigid ones. You can have fun with a vibrator, as it does a lot of the work for you and, indeed, can provide stronger simulation than your fingers. Rather than putting the vibrator directly into the vagina (which is not really going to do very much for you), vary the use by playing it around the clitoral area and putting it in and out of the vagina. Again, this teasing effect can produce good results.

Vibrators

For most women, regular vibrators work very well, but some women need something even stronger and, rather than a battery operated one, use something that is on a charger from the electrical mains. Some of the body massagers, which are electrically charged, produce great results. Don't be afraid to let go. That is what orgasm is all about and you have to be comfortable with letting go by yourself before you can let go in front of another person.

This was the case with Noreen, who I counselled over quite a long period. She had been trying for years to have an orgasm, without success, and blamed her husband Niall for her problems. I worked with her on her own and we looked at how she operated within her family and with other people. She was a controller and found it hard to let go on even simple things. She was constantly striving to keep things in order. Nobody could do things the way she liked them to be done, she kept an incredibly tidy house and a tight rein on everybody and everything.

I started to encourage her not to be so house proud, to make time for doing things she liked to do and to take on board the concept of 'good enough', rather than insisting that everything be perfect. She worked hard at this alongside doing the exercises and eventually she reached her goal of having an orgasm. She was tremendously excited by her results and took lots of time off from her household chores in order to enjoy her newly found skills. Eventually her husband complained to me that, because I had encouraged her to do things that she enjoyed, and she particularly enjoyed making bread, he was coming home to an extremely untidy house with lots and lots of freshly baked bread filling the kitchen and not much else in the way of food. I must say I thought it was worth it just to witness the smile on her face.

Orgasm with a partner

Now that you have learned how to orgasm, it is not such a big step to have one with your partner. If you are prepared to show him how you reach orgasm on your own through masturbation then that is the next step, but many women are too shy to do this. If this is the case you will have to teach him by having his hand on yours when you bring yourself to climax or by telling him what you want him to do. After you have done it once you will feel much freer the next time and gradually be able to experiment.

Trying to have an orgasm during intercourse is the next step and trying different positions can give interesting results. Remember, however, that you will probably need the additional stimulation of the clitoris by one or other of you in order to achieve orgasm. So if you are on top, your partner is easily able to stimulate your clitoris. Then, if you stretch your legs down straight so that they are on top of his, this will give more intense sensations. If you are feeling adventurous, get your partner to lie down flat on his back while you sit on his erect penis but facing away. Then lean backwards, keeping the penis inside you, which can be a bit tricky, but keep at it and you will be rewarded with some really nice sensations. At the same time both of you are free to stimulate the clitoris and this, added to the full feeling in the vagina, may well bring you to orgasm.

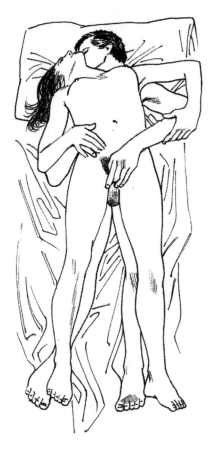

Figure 10
Woman on top, leaning back.

If you prefer the man on top, then adjust the missionary position a little so that he is further up the bed than he usually is. Because of this his penis won't go in all the way and the base of it will rub against the clitoris, which is what you need.

There are lots of possibilities – don't be afraid to try various things until you get what you want.

If you find the vibrator works for you, then how about including your partner in the experience. Again you may feel shy about this, but remember that men usually love a toy and most likely he will be very willing to participate. Whatever happens, you should have some fun in the trying and feel a lot closer as a result.

[7]

LACK
OF DESIRE

Of all the sexual problems that I am presented with, lack of desire is the one I feel to be the most complicated. It's like peeling an onion – as soon as you uncover one layer there is another one waiting to be uncovered.

I remember Carole and Joseph, who came to me for counselling for almost a year because of a lack of desire on her part. Their relationship was really great. As they had no children and worked together, they saw an awful lot of each other, but this was not a problem. They had evolved a way of living that worked for them, even taking it in turns – week on, week off – to do the household chores and the shopping. However Carole had very few sexual feelings and, while the act itself was fine for her when she got around to it, she never initiated it and never missed it if they had not had sex for a long time. Joseph was a fairly laid-back guy but the lack of intimacy bothered him greatly.

We spent a long time together at the sensate focus stage during which they were just giving and receiving massage. As this was a very intimate, but non-threatening exercise, it allowed Carole to start questioning her attitude to sex and her attitude towards a lot of things in her life. Our sessions together were extremely thought provoking and interesting as she worked through issues regarding previous lovers, her view on sex generally and her relationship with her mother. This led on to her questioning her own role as a mother and her reasons for shying away from becoming pregnant – having very infrequent sex was one of the ways she was doing this. Eventually she came to the conclusion that her own mother had very high standards and had always been very hard on Carole. If she herself became a mother would she be able to meet those very high standards? Also, would she be able to please her mother? As a result of this self-questioning, Carole had some in-depth conversations with her mother for the first time and was able to let go of a lot of things that had been bothering her. She also liked the concept of being 'good enough' rather than trying to be the best.

By now Carole was beginning to feel better about herself, and started to take more interest in sex. Some months later, she wrote to tell me that they were now being more sexual than they had been previously and what was particularly important to her was that on the last three occasions *she* was the one who had initiated it.

Below are some of the reasons for lack of desire.

Relationship difficulties

Problems within the relationship seem to me to be a major factor in lack of desire. When a couple are not getting on well together then chances are that sex is not happening either. This manifests itself in sexual withdrawal, more often on the woman's part than the man's. For instance, the woman will complain that her partner sees sex as a way of ending a row whereas she feels she cannot allow him near her until the argument as been resolved. Often, too, a woman will feel that, when she is unhappy in the relationship, the only part of her that she can keep to herself is her sexuality and so she withholds it.

I will never take a couple into sex therapy if I feel that their relationship is not good. I don't mean walking-off-into-the-sunset-happy-ever-after sort of good, but the aforementioned 'good enough'. I would suggest to a couple that they need some relationship counselling and that we can come back to the sexual problem when the relationship itself is in a healthier state.

If you are experiencing relationship difficulties that you feel are too big for you to handle by yourselves, I strongly advocate counselling. Well I would, wouldn't I, but I have seen the benefit it has had for people. Be careful which counsellor you choose and check their credentials. A good source of counsellors is from the Irish Association for Counselling and Therapy, 8 Cumberland Street, Dún Laoghaire, County Dublin. It has very strict accreditation criteria, which is very important as anybody can call themselves a counsellor and it is really vital that people are properly qualified.

Work-related tiredness

Our vibrant economy and newfound prosperity has to have a downside, and it does. Tiredness. Young couples are working very hard, both of them, starting earlier and earlier each morning as they commute longer distances. They have enormous mortgages and so the possibility of one of them stopping work is not an option. They work late in order to avoid very bad traffic problems; the workplace itself is often a very stressful environment and, by the time they get home, they are exhausted. All they want to do is eat and sleep and perhaps watch the television for a while. They simply do not have the energy for sex. Also, because of working long hours, some couples are not able to spend very much time together and, as a result, lose some of the closeness that they had earlier enjoyed.

Fear of intimacy

Some people really *do* fear intimacy. Perhaps they never had it in their earlier lives and the feeling makes them very uncomfortable or maybe they do not want to get too close to their partner thereby becoming vulnerable and needy.

Such was the case with Patricia and Edward, who I counselled because of Patricia's lack of desire. She maintained that, with two small children and a full-time senior position in her firm, she was simply very tired and in the evenings all she wanted to do was to get the children to bed, read for a little while and then go to bed herself. Sleep became the most important thing in her life. Edward, however, did not believe that this was the case and felt that there was some deeper cause. He told me that he had taken to staying up late, playing his guitar, so that she would be asleep when he got to bed and would not have to face rejection. They were very much in love, but the sexual problem was causing them a lot of unhappiness.

We started into the sensate focus exercises and what a revelation that was! The very first week, they came back to me to tell me that the exercises had been an absolute disaster. They had done the exercise only once and, as instructed, had each given the other a massage in a non-sexual way, avoiding the breasts and the genital area, having first set the mood with a bath, some relaxing music and lighting. Edward had become overwhelmed with a feeling of sadness, so much so that he had not been able to do the other sessions I had asked of them. We talked about this at length and he was able to relate his feelings during the massage to those he experienced when he was at boarding school. When he had been there he had been tremendously lonely and had taken refuge in his room with his guitar when things got too rough. When he was with Patricia, he started to remember all the lonely evenings he had had – first in school and then at home – and the intimacy he was now having was so different to all of that, that he was unable to handle it. So it transpired that, in fact, it had been Edward's lack of desire all along that had been the problem. We stayed quite a long time at this point in the therapy until he was comfortable with the good feelings that intimacy produced.

Hygiene

The first thing we usually do when we are getting ready to go on an important date, attend an interview, go out to dinner, and so on, is to shower or have a bath, and shave, in the man's case, or apply make-up, in the woman's. So what is the message our partner gets if we expect to be sexual with them and yet we are unwashed, unshaven, have lank hair, smell of the pub or of cigarettes or curry (or all three)? I would suggest that it tells them that we don't think much of them and that we feel that it is our right to have sex no matter what physical state we are in.

Hygiene is an issue that comes up again and again in my sessions with clients, and I find that people are much more inclined to discuss hygiene issues when they are on their own. It is almost as if they are afraid to discuss it with their partner. One woman was absolutely horrified when I suggested that she tell her husband that she would like him to brush his teeth when he wanted to have sex with her. She did not feel it was her right to do so and she was afraid of what he might say to her. In a way, that spoke volumes about the relationship itself, but, nevertheless sometimes these things need to be said.

When a couple are in therapy the very first thing they are instructed to do is to have a bath or a shower so that they are refreshed and also have a lovely clean body with which to work. In the past, when there was no central heating and bath time on Saturday night (or before Sunday morning mass) involved boiling endless kettles of water or, in later years, turning on the immersion heater, things were very difficult. I also feel that with all our modern day conveniences I should not have to be writing this paragraph. But the evidence from some clients shows that it still needs to be said. When we are discussing oral sex in particular, a subject on which people have very strong views, hygiene is often given as a reason for either not allowing it or not giving it.

In all sort of ways, the lack of personal hygiene can lead to a lack of desire in one's partner. So examine your conscience if it needs to be examined and you will reap the benefits.

Children

Throughout the different stages in their lives, children can be responsible for a lack of desire in either partner. In fact, even when the couple are trying to conceive a child, particularly if they are in some form of human-assisted reproduction programme, they may rebel against having to perform on demand and may go off sex completely.

In their early years, children often deprive their parents of adequate sleep, which can lead to a loss of desire. As infants get a little older and learn to walk, they often end up coming into the parental bed and, in order to get a night's sleep, the parents allow them to stay. This is a very dangerous practise and I have heard some horror stories of the kids still coming into the bed at night, aged seven or eight, and real problems ensue trying to break the habit. It can also cause big problems within the couple's relationship, as one parent is often much softer with the child and allows the behaviour to continue, which could lead to feelings of resentment from the other partner.

When children are in their early teens, a lot of people tell me that they are aware that their children are awake in the next bedroom and they feel very inhibited in their lovemaking in case they will be heard. Their desire for sex diminishes as they begin to associate it with negative feelings and it becomes a

LACK OF DESIRE

hassle for them. As in most things sexual, this is usually the case with one parent only and this, in turn, leads to conflict.

Different sexual appetites

It is extremely rare for a couple to have the same level of sexual appetite and this inevitably causes problems. In terms of percentages, it is more often the man who has the greater desire for sex, but it can often be the woman who complains that she is not getting enough to satisfy her. Sometimes I daydream about putting various clients together with matching appetites to see what the results would be but, of course, it remains a daydream! Given that it is almost always the case that there are different levels of desire within any relationship, it is what the couple do about this that holds the solution. Just because the man wants sex every night does not mean that he is entitled to it, any more than a woman who would be satisfied with it once a fortnight is entitled to *that*. Neither is right and neither is to blame. So, as in most areas in relationships, compromise has to be reached.

I often suggest different solutions that the couple might try. In the above case of every night as opposed to once a fortnight, how about settling for a few times a week? Or what if the person who is refusing suggests another definite time instead, and it becomes a case of, "I'm really not in the mood right now but how about we go to bed early on Friday night instead?" In this way, the initiator does not feel rejected. The couple could try taking turns – week on, week off – so that each has their wish for a full week and the partner agrees to whatever they want, and vice versa. Different ways should be explored until a couple finds what is right for them.

Different levels of desire are a very frequent problem and, if left untreated, can have disastrous results. This was the case when Imelda and Pat came to see me. Imelda had had a very low libido ever since their children had arrived. She was a very

121

beautiful woman and Pat spoke very passionately about how he felt watching her at different times – coming out of the shower, getting dressed to go out, coming to bed, getting up out of bed – and about how much he wanted her. However, he was constantly rejected. He got so used to the rejection that it, eventually, took its toll and he did not desire her anymore, to the extent that he was now getting out of the marriage. He was filled with resentment that, sexually, she had taken away the last ten years of his life, and, as he was now forty, he had no intention of losing the coming decades, too. I saw them both together and on their own and he was absolutely adamant he wanted to get out of the relationship. By now Imelda was prepared to do anything to keep him, but sadly it was too late. There was nothing that could be done and he left her. She continued coming to see me for some time and her constant refrain was, "If only I had done something earlier about my lack of desire I could have avoided all of this pain."

Boredom

I think that it is quite normal if you don't feel desire for your partner all the time, particularly if you have been lovers for years. It is somewhat unrealistic to expect sex always to be passionate and full of thrills when you know each other inside out! So some times sex will be better than others – the bread-and-butter kind as opposed to the cordon bleu. However, there is often a tendency not to have any variety on the basis of if-it's-not-broken-why-mend-it, whereas even a little thing like trying a new position or changing the venue can make a difference.

Medical problems

Any medical condition, whether acute or ongoing, is bound to cause a decrease in sexual desire. This stands to reason, as an illness can become the most important factor in a person's life, particularly if it is major and necessitates treatment in the form of surgery, radiation, drugs, and so on. However, there are other medical issues besides illness to consider.

- **LOW HORMONE LEVELS**

  Testosterone is the hormone that controls the desire in both men and women and, if you feel that you have no desire whatsoever and no sexual thoughts or fantasies, not necessarily only about your partner, then have your testosterone level checked by your GP.

- **DEPRESSION**

  If somebody comes to me suffering from depression, I will not take them into treatment unless the depression is treated first. Loss of interest in sex as a result of depression is normal and sexual therapy will not work until the depression is treated.

- **DRUGS**

  The lowering of libido is a side-effect of quite a number of drugs. For example, people who are on regular sleeping tablets may experience lack of desire but not associate that with their medication. If you feel that medication is to blame for your lack of desire, you should get your doctor to check if they can prescribe another drug that can do the same thing but without the loss of desire.

So you see, there can be all sorts of reasons for a lack of desire, and sometimes it can be a combination of a number of these factors. Bear in mind that everybody goes through peaks and valleys in their sex lives and often there is no need to worry.

A rule of thumb should be that if a problem continues for six months or more then it is time to seek help.

[8]

CONTRACEPTION

In my experience, the cause of a lot of sexual problems is simply a fear of pregnancy. There are so many different types of contraception available and yet I often come across couples who are not using any at all and it never ceases to amaze me. Please be aware that it is not necessary to have sexual intercourse in order to become pregnant. Some of those sperm are incredibly good swimmers and when you consider that the average ejaculate of five millilitres contains three hundred million sperm, there is a pretty good chance that *one* of them will get where it wants to go. I have had a few clients who suffered from vaginismus (where she cannot allow penetration) and yet had a couple of children having become pregnant when the ejaculate was deposited around the entrance to the vagina. If either person in a couple is a bit anxious that a pregnancy may occur, it stands to reason that they will not be as relaxed as they should be in their lovemaking and problems such as dyspareunia (painful intercourse), vaginismus, lack of desire, and erectile and ejaculatory problems can result. So never underestimate the power of the fear of pregnancy as a factor.

There are three basic types of contraception available as well as natural family planning and sterilisation.

* *Barrier methods*, such as male and female condoms and caps.

- *Hormonal methods*, there are many varieties of 'the pill' available and there are also those given by injection. (There is also an intrauterine device that releases hormones locally.)

- *Intrauterine devices or IUDs.*

Barrier methods

These are designed to act as physical barriers against sperm, preventing it having any contact with a possible egg that might be present in the womb.

CONDOMS

The most popular barrier method of contraception is the condom, which not alone acts as a contraceptive, but also gives protection against sexually transmitted diseases. Condoms are made of rubber and made to cover the erect penis and so prevent the passage of sperm into the vagina. They come in different sizes and, if you are using them on a regular basis, it is a good idea to shop around until you find one that suits you. Men have told me they stopped using condoms because they found them uncomfortable having been unaware that there were different sizes available. Condoms are very useful as they require no pre-planning – other than having one to hand when required – but they are not 100 per cent safe.

Apart from being good protection against sexually transmitted diseases, condoms are suitable for those who dislike the messiness of semen. This is an advantage from the woman's point of view in that she does not experience any of the 'leaking' sensation that occurs for some time after lovemaking, often when she is least expecting it.

Below are some common errors in the use of condoms.

Genital contact before the condom has been put on
When the man has already reached high arousal there may be a little piece of what seems to be ejaculate at the tip of the penis.

This is a secretion called the Cowper's Gland secretion and, if some sperm is still present in the urethra from previous intercourse or masturbation, the secretion will contain this sperm. So although the man puts the condom on before coming, the sperm has already been deposited in the vagina and so a pregnancy can occur. This happens more often than people realise.

Leakage due to loss of erection
This can happen particularly if the man is a bit anxious. In this case, the condom can slip off unnoticed – don't forget the woman has very little sensation in the vagina and so will not feel the condom slipping off – and ejaculation may occur. It is possible to ejaculate with a flaccid penis, so be careful.

Leakage of the ejaculate on withdrawal
Again this can occur particularly if the penis has become flaccid. It is best to withdraw very quickly after ejaculation.

Damage to the condom
Fingernails and chemicals, such as those found in many vaginal preparations, can seriously damage condoms and cause tiny tears in them. Baby oil, for instance, destroys 90 per cent of the condom's strength after fifteen minutes' contact. When condoms are being used, additional safety can be added if the woman inserts into her vagina a spermicidal sponge or pessary, available in any pharmacy.

FEMIDOM
Femidom is the only female condom on the market. It works on the same principle as the male condom but is inserted into the vagina before intercourse. A much larger device than its male counterpart, the Femidom is seventeen centimetres long with an inner and outer ring, six centimetres and seven centimetres, respectively. It is already pre-loaded with a lubricant and more or less forms a well-lubricated secondary vagina.

They are more expensive than male condoms and can be seen at the entrance to the vagina when in place. The advantages of Femidoms are that they are under the woman's control, they do not slip out of place, they are very effective against infection and they allow male sensations to be more normal than with a male condom.

OCCLUSIVE CAP OR DIAPHRAGM

These apparently date from 1850 BC and were first made from crocodile dung in ancient Egypt! Now they are made from latex. They lie diagonally across the cervix (the neck of the womb) and are used together with a spermicidal jelly, which is smeared around the rim of the cap.

Expert instruction is needed in order to learn how to use the cap, but everybody manages it in the end. It is put in before intercourse and must be kept in place for at least six to eight hours afterwards.

Further intercourse on the same occasion has to be covered by the insertion of more spermicide. It is a very safe method of contraception, from the point of view of the

Figure 11
Diaphragm.

health of the woman, and is reasonably effective if used conscientiously and in combination with the spermicidal cream. It is a good method to use if a woman is not sexually active very often as, for the rest of the time, there is no chemical interference with her body. Many women dislike it, however, as they do not like the frequent handling of their own genitalia. Sometimes the male partner finds the diaphragm uncomfortable during intercourse and if the woman has a weight gain of more than three kilograms a re-fitting session with her doctor will be necessary. Urinary tract infections are a rare complication caused by the pressure of the rim of the diaphragm on the urethra.

Hormonal methods

HORMONAL PILLS

The pill works by mimicking the effect pregnancy has on a woman's body. By taking a contraceptive pill every day, the woman keeps a constant stream of hormones in her bloodstream that prevents her getting pregnant in the same way as her natural hormones would prevent conception if she were already pregnant. This works in three ways:

- no egg is released that could be fertilised by sperm;
- the fluid in the neck of the womb thickens, making it more difficult for sperm to enter; and
- the lining of the womb does not thicken enough for the egg to grow in it.

All of these effects stop when the woman ceases taking the pill.

There are a variety of pills on the market and they are made up of varying combinations of the female hormones, progesterone and oestrogen. Your doctor will advise you about which pill would be best suited to your individual needs.

There are also injections available that do the same thing as the contraceptive pill and they are administered every two or three months. The primary action is to prevent ovulation and cervical mucus thickening helps this. They contain only progesterone so there are none of the clotting risks that are associated with the pill, particularly for smokers. Irregular bleeding can occur at the start of treatment, but usually stops after two injections. Eventually there is no bleeding at all, which can be very beneficial and liberating for the woman.

All hormonal methods have to be monitored for side effects and the most common side effects I have found with clients on the pill are weight gain, headaches and loss of desire. Sexually this can lead to problems but it is important that you discuss this with your doctor and be prepared to try a few different pills in order to find one that suits you. The advantages of the hormonal method of contraception are that it is very simple just to take a pill every day or have an injection every couple of months. It also means that the woman is always prepared, contraception-wise, for lovemaking and her periods are much lighter.

THE MORNING-AFTER PILL

The morning-after pill, as it is known, is also available, although this should come under the heading of *emergency contraception*. Ever since the discovery that semen was responsible for fertilisation, women have used some form of emergency contraception. Douching – whereby a variety of liquids are inserted in the vagina to try and prevent fertilisation occurring – has been used since ancient times. These liquids have included everything from the mixture of wine, garlic and fennel, used in Ancient Egypt, to reports, in more recent times, of some misguided people using Coca Cola. Needless to say, failure rates were high.

Nowadays the method is to take two tablets of Ovran 50 together with one Stemetil and repeat the dose twelve hours later. The tablets should be taken as soon as possible after unprotected intercourse and can be taken up to seventy-two hours after the event with a high rate of success. Two weeks later a pregnancy test is carried out to check that it has worked. The reason for waiting for two weeks is that this time span is necessary for the pregnancy test to be valid. No intercourse should take place during those two weeks. A few days after taking the pills there may be a small amount of bleeding. This is a withdrawal bleed, due to the stopping of the hormones, and not a period. The follow up visit to the doctor, who prescribed the medication, should include a discussion as to what form of contraception would be most suitable for the future. Though the morning-after pill is a very good standby to have around in the case of condom leakage, carelessness (perhaps due to alcohol consumption) or in the aftermath of a rape; it should not be used as a continuing form of contraception.

A newspaper article I read some time ago said that a lot of the family planning clinics in Dublin noted a sharp increase in the demand for the morning-after pill on the Mondays following a rugby international. No such demand was noted after football finals. Draw your own conclusions!

Intrauterine devices or IUDs

An intrauterine device is any object that is inserted via the cervical canal and retained in the uterus for the purpose of preventing pregnancy. They have threads attached that act as markers and these can be seen at the entrance to the womb. There are two main types of IUDs: copper bearing and hormone releasing.

Intrauterine devices were used over 2,500 years ago by Hippocrates, the physician of Ancient Greece, commonly regarded as the father of medicine. However, it is not clear for what purpose. Casanova, an Italian famous for his sexual adventures, is supposed to have recommended a gold ball! In the late-19th century they were made from a variety of materials including glass, ivory and diamond-studded platinum. Although initially they were inserted to act as a barrier, it was learned that when they broke, the piece that stayed behind in the uterus acted as a contraceptive. Many of the earlier devices were used as abortifacients (devices to cause abortion) as well as contraceptives, and often resulted in haemorrhage and pelvic infection.

IUDs have to be fitted by an expert and they act in different ways to prevent pregnancy. The 'Copper T', for instance, causes an inflammatory reaction in the cells of the genital tract, which impedes sperm transport and fertilisation.

Mirena is an IUD made of plastic that releases hormones to stop the sperm reaching the egg – the hormones inhibit the normal sperm function inside the womb and thicken the mucus in the cervix. Its disadvantages are some spotting or light bleeding in addition to the normal periods for the first three months after the system is fitted. Its advantage, however, is that once it is fitted it can be forgotten.

Natural methods

In 1968, in its encyclical *Humanae Vitae*, the Roman Catholic Church deemed any artificial method of avoiding conception to be immoral and the current Pope has continually reiterated this opinion. As a consequence, various rhythm methods, which avoid intercourse during the fertile period of the woman's cycle, are the only methods of fertility control acceptable to the Catholic Church, at least in its public pronouncements. (Many individual priests will disagree in private with the Church's view.)

The two most common natural methods are, firstly, taking a daily temperature and working out the day of ovulation by the rise in temperature; and secondly, a method whereby the woman learns how to recognise the changes in her cervical mucus and by so doing gets to know when she is nearing ovulation. This second method is called the Billings method. Intercourse is then avoided until the so-called safe period.

In the Billings method, the woman is told to observe the quantity, fluidity, transparency, tenacity and shine of the cervical mucus every day. She records this in a diary. Before ovulation the mucus tends to be slippery and transparent and very tenacious and resembles beaten eggwhite. After ovulation it reduces in quantity and is sticky and opaque. Intercourse is avoided during the days when there is a lot of mucus and for four days after. However, the fluid of sexual arousal and semen can confuse things and vaginal infection can also distort the picture. So, from a practical point of view, measuring mucus is not an easy business. It is all very well in theory, but very often in practise it does not work.

I remember being in a maternity hospital having just had a baby and someone opened my door. A woman put her head in and told me she wanted to show me something. She brought me over to her room and said, "I want to show you a Billings baby!" and there was a lovely baby gurgling up at us.

For either of these methods to work satisfactorily, an awful lot of abstinence is required, which may not suit a couple's lifestyle or mood. Rhythm methods also need the couple to abstain from sexual intercourse at a time when the woman's sexual desire is usually at its peak. Moreover, there can be a lot of human error with regard to the 'safe period' and it can cause a lot of tension within the relationship. However, for the couple who want to keep to their Church's teaching it has the advantage of not having any chemical or medical intervention.

Coitus interruptus

The deliberate withdrawal of the penis from the vagina before ejaculation is sometimes used as a method of birth control. However, I have not included it in my list of birth control methods, as to my mind, it is simply not a viable means of contraception. It shows great irresponsibility to rely on it as method of avoiding pregnancy. Moreover, it gives an altogether incomplete and unsatisfactory ending to what should be a joyful act.

As a conclusion to this section on contraception, I cannot emphasise strongly enough the extent to which a worry about becoming pregnant can influence the enjoyment level and spontaneity of making love, so be prepared and you will enjoy the act even more.

Sterilisation

Another means of contraception available to a couple is either male or female sterilisation, which is a permanent way of controlling conception.

VASECTOMY

Male sterilisation is a quick and simple surgical procedure, called a vasectomy, done under local anaesthetic. It involves making a cut in the vas deferens (the sperm-bearing duct) so that the sperm is unable to continue its journey. However, this does not interfere with the ejaculatory process so the man does not feel any different when making love. It is, however, practically irreversible and, therefore, it goes without saying that a lot of thought should go into taking the decision to have a vasectomy. Some men fear that after the procedure they will have fewer sensations, or that their erections will not be as firm. Let me reassure any man considering a vasectomy that there is absolutely no physiological reason for either of these things to happen.

TUBAL LIGATION

The female equivalent of a vasectomy is tubal ligation. In this procedure, clips or rings are inserted through a laparoscope and applied to the fallopian tubes. This is done under general anaesthetic and, as with any surgery, has its associated dangers. It, too, is largely irreversible and there is some evidence that heavier periods can ensue following this operation, so again, it is not a decision that should be taken lightly.

This is the range of options that are available concerning contraception and given the variety I think there is something to suit everybody and every situation.

[9]

HUMAN-ASSISTED REPRODUCTION

For people who have no difficulty in becoming pregnant it is probably hard to imagine the feelings of those who are not successful in achieving a pregnancy. Couples who are infertile speak of the mixed emotions they experience when a close relative or friend announces a pregnancy or gives birth; they are happy for their friends but very sad for themselves. Every advertisement on television connected to children serves to remind them that parenthood is not possible for them. There are a myriad of things that keeps their infertility in the forefront of their minds, among them the well-intentioned, but devastating, enquiries from friends as to when they are going to start a family, or just walking past the baby-section in a shop. One woman told me that every single time she looks at the tampon machine in the Ladies' Room at work she is reminded that she has a period every month and cannot get pregnant.

Among the options open to these couples are adoption, long-term fostering and infertility investigation treatment. This latter may, at the end of the line, include human-assisted reproduction – what used to be called 'test tube babies'. As any decision that affects the rest of their lives needs careful consideration, it is vital that partners are in agreement with, and fully understand, the implications of their chosen route.

As people have a somewhat hazy idea as to what human-assisted reproduction entails, I will concentrate on the procedures and I will try as far as possible to use non-medical terms.

Any couple going for fertility treatment will first go to their GP for tests, as the results of these tests and a referral letter will need to be supplied to whatever clinic they will be attending. The GP will do a rubella screening and smear test on the woman, if she has not had one in the last two years, and she will be advised to commence taking folic acid and vitamin B12. Her partner will usually have a sperm count done at this time also.

It is important for a couple to realise that, when they start investigating the reasons for their infertility, there is a strong possibility that one of them will have a physical reason – whether it is blocked fallopian tubes, low sperm count, not producing eggs or any of a number of other factors causing the infertility. This realisation can bring with it huge guilt, pain, loss of self-esteem and feelings of failure so, before any tests are done, the couple would be well advised to talk this eventuality through in order to be prepared for the strong emotions that may be unleashed. Of course, there can also be unexplained infertility where no valid reason can be found, in which case, neither party feels particularly to blame.

Infertility treatment can have an enormous effect on couples in all sorts of ways – emotionally and physically, even socially – as they try to fit in the various commitments that are required of them once treatment starts. It may even cause problems with intercourse, particularly on the male side, leading to erectile difficulties. It is, therefore, necessary that the time is right for a couple to start treatment and that nothing else is happening in their lives that could add to the stresses that they will undoubtedly encounter. It's not that I want to paint a gloomy picture, but I feel that before a couple undertakes infertility treatment every effort should be made to ensure that things have the very best chance of working out well.

Human-assisted reproduction is often called IVF (which means in vitro fertilisation) or ICSI (which stands for intra-cytoplasmic sperm injection). Both these methods involve the removal of ripe eggs from the ovary through the vagina and the subsequent fertilisation of these eggs by the male sperm, which the man has produced through masturbation. The difference between IVF and ICSI is the method used in the laboratory. In the former, the sperms are put close to the egg and they swim into it. In the latter, a single motile sperm is selected for injection directly into the egg.

The couple go through the same procedures for both IVF and ICSI. In each case, the fertilised eggs are put into the womb through the cervix, or neck of the womb, and then nature takes over and the egg continues to grow and develop.

When the couple are accepted on to a treatment programme they should expect the procedure to last roughly six weeks, divided into three two-week sections.

SECTION ONE
Having had a pre-period scan, which is done by passing a probe into the vagina in a painless procedure so that the womb and ovaries can be checked, the woman will be given a special nasal spray and instructed to start using it on day one of her period. This has to be used every six hours for fourteen days and the purpose of this is to shut down the normal hormonal activity in order to prepare her ovaries for the next phase of the treatment. On day fourteen, she has another scan and a blood test to check the hormone levels. If all is well, she proceeds to Section Two.

SECTION TWO
The woman will have daily injections for an average of ten days. These injections are given by a GP or trained nurse. On day seven of the injections, a scan is taken to see how the ovaries are responding to the injections. Hopefully, follicles are developing on both ovaries. Each follicle is a fluid-filled sac containing a growing egg. A blood test is also taken to check

hormone levels. Meanwhile, the laboratory will be preparing a solution to store the eggs in when they have been collected. On day ten, if all is going well, there is another scan and a blood test. After that there will be a scan and blood test every day until the follicles have reached a particular size and the woman is ready for egg collection. When this happens, stimulation injections are stopped and she is told not to use the nasal spray.

Later that evening, the woman will get an injection to prepare the eggs for collection. Thirty-four hours after this injection, the egg collection will be done so that there is a free day in between. While this is happening, the woman will be sedated but not fully asleep, scanned in the usual way and a needle, which is attached to a vaginal probe, is guided into each ovary. The eggs are collected by draining the fluid from each follicle. This procedure takes around forty minutes.

Around the same time, the husband will be asked to give a semen sample. This can cause problems for some men, as it can be difficult to supply what amounts to ejaculation on demand. However, special arrangements can be made to help a man with this, and in some cases there is a possibility of freezing some sperm in advance to have a back-up.

The laboratory then takes over and, hopefully, fertilisation should take place in the next twelve to fifteen hours. The zygotes, as they are then called, will be transferred the following day into the womb through a thin plastic tube. This is similar to a smear test and does not involve an anaesthetic.

SECTION THREE
The couple now have to wait to see if the procedure has been successful. This is a very difficult time with lots of different emotions. If the woman gets to day sixteen without a bleed, a pregnancy test can be done. If she has a period, then it means she is not pregnant and that realisation can bring with it immense disappointment.

If the procedure hasn't worked and so the woman is not pregnant, this is an incredibly difficult time for the prospective parents – all their dreams have come to nothing and, if they start all over again, they have no guarantee that it will work the next time. They have probably told a few close friends or family about the programme they are going through and they have to tell them the bad news as well. Throughout the treatment the couple can avail of counselling, and this counselling is absolutely necessary if the procedure has failed and the couple are working their way through the grief process of what might have been.

If, on the other hand, the pregnancy test is positive, the woman will be scanned three weeks later. By this time she will be seven weeks pregnant and delighted with the outcome of all the hard work she and her partner have done.

I have based all my information on the excellent work done by Professor R Harrison and his team at the HARI Unit in the Rotunda Hospital, Dublin.

[10]

SEX AND
DISABILITY

In our modern world, sex is often associated with youth
and physical fitness – the perfect body that the media
encourages us all to strive for. Therefore, society tends to
view people with disability as non-sexual. This is simply not
the case – a person with a disability, male or a female, is also a
sexual being regardless of their physical or mental state. As well
as their disability they have the added burden of belonging to
a minority and have to overcome other people's prejudices and
misconceptions regarding their sexuality, among other things.
I remember a friend of mine who was wheelchair bound after a
car accident. "Does he take sugar?" became his catchphrase
because whoever was accompanying him was asked that question
time and time again. In a lot of people's eyes, the fact that he was
in a wheelchair meant he was without the power of speech too.

My main experience in working in the area of disability has
been working with ostomates – that is, people who have
undergone ostomy surgery – and so I am going to talk about
this particular form of disability. However, what I say can, in
turn, be applied to various other forms of disability and it may
help those of you fortunate enough not to be disabled to get
an idea of what disabled people have to go through.

An ostomy is where there is an artificial stoma, or opening, into
a urinary or gastrointestinal canal, or the trachea (windpipe).

Ostomy surgery in the urinary or gastrointestinal canal necessitates a bag being worn outside of the body to collect waste matter.

Ostomy surgery is about change in your body, a change you did not want or ask for. Even if it brought to an end an awful lot of illness and discomfort, or has been done to cure a life-threatening disease, it still represents the loss of a natural bodily function and the acquisition of a new body part. You are forced into dealing with your body in new ways and into talking about things you never had to talk about before. Your sexuality is one of those things. Ostomy surgery involves a major change in your body, and change is very frightening.

I often say to clients that even something as simple as going to the hairdresser and finding that the person who usually cuts your hair is out sick can be quite scary. We will often opt for a blow dry only and then wait until our regular stylist comes back rather than have somebody else cut our hair. And, in this case, it is a very minor change we are talking about. Another example is that if somebody sits at our place at the kitchen table we can feel uncomfortable at having to sit somewhere else – again a very insignificant change, but one that has an effect on us. After ostomy surgery you are looking at major changes in body image and in sexual relations with a partner. Lots of new feelings may be awakened.

In some ways, I would liken what happens to a death and the resulting grieving process. Those of you who have experienced the death of a loved one will be able to recognise the various stages that one goes through. First there is the shock of the death (or in this case the diagnosis). Then there is the anger and blame: if only the ambulance had been quicker; if only the weather had not been so bad, the crash would not have happened; if only the diagnosis had been reached earlier.

Then anger kicks in and it can be directed at God, the medical profession, the causes of stress; in fact, at anything that relieves the anger. Anger at being ill and at having to go through surgery is very natural.

Anger and fear are very closely related and fear, in this case, is the fear of the unknown. You may fear the loss of your bodily function, your loved ones or your life. When a loved one dies there is fear as to what the future will be like without that person. "How am I ever going to cope without them?" is a question that is asked over and over again.

Since sex is intimately tied up with our most important feelings about ourselves, it is crucial that these feelings of fear and anger about your sexuality, and fear of losing it, are worked through, either on your own or with your partner or a trusted friend. When these issues are not expressed in some way, they can lead to resentment, rejection and physical and emotional distance from the people about whom you care the most.

The next stage in the grieving process is occasionally forgetting that the person is gone. You can find yourself reaching for the telephone to tell them something, setting a place for them at the table or listening for their car outside, until with a sickening thud you realise that they are no longer with you. This lapse of memory, I would imagine, can sometimes happen to the ostomate as well, but then the realisation of the change that has taken place in their body dawns again.

This brings us onto the next phase, the gradual acceptance of the loss of the loved one. To my mind this is one of the hardest parts. The funeral is long since over, all the letters have been written, people are no longer calling to check if you are all right and life goes on in the new altered state. Likewise, in the case of the ostomate: the surgery is long since past, the life threatening or serious illness has abated, your strength has slowly returned and you begin to pick up the pieces of your life, albeit in its new altered state. Your appetite for food starts to return, and with it, sooner or later, your sexual appetite.

Sexuality *is* an appetite and I often liken it to our appetite for food. For instance, sometimes we would like a big four-course meal and sometimes just a sandwich. Sometimes we would like a long sex session, sometimes a quickie is much more fun!

Your sexual appetite is usually one of the first appetites to vanish when you are in pain, anxious, depressed or grieving. When you are rested, healed and reassured, your appetite returns. If your surgery has been very recent, you may still be healing, still experiencing loss and your sexual appetite may not have returned yet. It is important that you take your time and are patient and kind with yourself. Grief takes its own time, and fortunately it *does* heal with time no matter what the source of the loss is.

So what about sex and the ostomate? The most important sex organ that you bring to love making is not the penis, the clitoris or the vagina, but the *brain*. That is where most sexual difficulties start and indeed where a lot of them can be solved. I never cease to be amazed at just how strong an influence the brain can have on the body.

One of the most common sexual dysfunctions in the female is vaginismus, discussed in *Chapter 5*, an involuntary spasm of the muscles at the entrance to the vagina that is caused entirely by the brain. Women who suffer from vaginismus will report all sorts of pain on attempting sexual intercourse and yet they usually end up having successful and enjoyable intercourse with no intervention other than talking to me, or another sex therapist, and doing prescribed exercises. The same is true of men with, amongst other things, erectile dysfunction. Having checked out that there is no physical cause for their problem, it is a source of joy to me to watch their self-esteem grow in direct relation to the functioning of their penis. This, again, is because their confidence has begun to return and their brain is allowing them to become sufficiently aroused to have an erection.

One surgeon lists four normal (and solvable) problems that may arise after surgery.

- Failure to have an erection or orgasm because of attempting intercourse before strength returns following the operation.

- Serious anxiety or fear about being able to perform sexually, or anxiety or fear about the attractiveness of one's altered body, or anxiety about the possibility of odour and the security of the appliance or stoma covering. I'm sure all these anxieties will ring bells for ostomates.

- Depression that many people suffer from following any surgery.

- Excessive medication that can lead to orgasmic difficulties. (At this point I might add that this applies to excessive intake of alcohol as well. Some of us may be familiar with the term 'brewer's droop' which obviously applies to men, but I do not think it is widely known that excessive alcohol causes problems with orgasms in women as well.)

Probably the most basic factor in sexual intimacy is liking one-self. The feeling of being a worthwhile person (with or without an ostomy) becomes contagious. If we feel good about ourselves, others feel good about us, too. If we accept an ostomy, others accept it, too. Even in ideal circumstances it takes time to become comfortable with an ostomy, to forget it some of the time, to return to being a person who just happens to have an ostomy rather than an ostomy with a person attached. Most people have doubts about themselves even before surgery, in fact most people have doubts about themselves all through their lives. I remember a very successful business manager who came to me for counselling. She gave the impression of being in total control of her life and yet when I got to know her, she admitted to being plagued with self doubts and constantly feared 'being found out', as she put it. It is keeping the doubts at an acceptable level that does the trick. In my experience, about 50 per cent of all couples report sexual difficulties of one kind or another and people with ostomies are no different.

I would like, now, to look at the male and females ostomates separately.

Female ostomates

I note that in the booklet *Going Home: Living with an Ileostomy* (Ileostomy and Internal Pouch Support Group, Scunthorpe, England, 1996), there are four lines devoted to female ostomates. Given how preoccupied women can be with their bodies and their unhappiness about various bits, four lines hardly seem sufficient. However, some women come to accept the altered state of their body completely. On holidays last year, I remember seeing a woman in her mid-60s, who had had a single mastectomy, sunbathing in just her bikini bottoms. It struck me that here was a woman who had come to accept her altered body to such a degree that she was happy not just to let her husband see her, but everybody else as well.

That is what I mean by accepting yourself and liking yourself. Just because you have an altered body does not mean that you have an altered personality as well. All the things that people loved about you, and all the things that irritated them pre-surgery, are still there.

I remember working with a couple who came to see me in total shock because they had just been told by their son that he was gay. Trying to help them get their heads around the fact that he was the same boy they had loved the day before he told them, took a lot of doing. So spend some time reminding yourself that this new you is still the same person you were before your operation.

A survey has been done of sixty-two female ostomates in which the last question they were asked was: "What would you tell another woman going through ostomy surgery if she asked you about sex?" Below is a list of their collective answers.

- Be a little careful at first, make sure you are with a good partner. It's not all easy, but not all ostomates have problems.

- Live fully, your attitude is important. Have fun and a sense of humour.

- Relax, be patient, accept your new self. You are not diminished as a person.

- Partners need help, too. How the partner accepts the ostomy is important.

- Given a good attitude and a positive outlook on sex before surgery, sex after surgery can be as good, or better.

There can be some physical problems for the women following ostomy surgery. The first of these is painful intercourse, or dyspareunia, to give it its official title. This can happen in particular after surgery involving removal of the rectum. Closure of the anus can cause a tightening and discomfort similar to that which any woman may experience during the first few times she has sexual intercourse. Gentle sexual activity involving a slow and gradual approach towards intercourse, fondling, masturbation and oral sex are some of the ways that might lessen the discomfort. It is very important to let your partner know what you are feeling as they simply cannot know unless you tell them. Resuming intercourse need not happen in one session. Indeed, if you think back to the beginning of any relationship, you will recall that usually you did not leap into bed and have sexual intercourse straightaway. Rather, it was a gradual process that eventually led to being fully sexual.

If painful intercourse persists, you should discuss this with a sensitive gynaecologist (your doctor should be able to refer you). And do not be afraid to consult more than one specialist if you don't feel comfortable with the first one you go to see – shop around if necessary. Remember it is *your* body and you owe it to yourself to give it your best care and attention.

You may experience a decrease in clitoral feeling and possibly in orgasm. Most of a woman's sensitivity is in her clitoris, which elongates and swells when she is aroused. However, just as the nerves to the penis may be damaged by cutting in surgery, so it is possible that nerves to the clitoris may also be damaged. You can understand that, as a result, there may be a reduction in clitoral feeling or in orgasm.

Problems with lubrication are common and can be due to a number of things, not least anxiety. There are some very good lubricants available, such as KY jelly, SYLK and Astraglide. Also experiment with positions. It may be that a position you previously did not like or did not even think of – like side-by-side – can now be very acceptable. And don't forget that cushions or pillows under the bottom can alter the tilt of your uterus and again provide relief from pain. Be creative and, above all, do not lose your sense of humour. Non-ostomates also have problems with things like breaking wind, belching and strange noises. I remember one couple, who I had been counselling for vaginismus, coming back to me as they were upset. It transpired that when they did, eventually, manage to get it together, they felt that they must be doing it wrong as there were all sorts of strange noises coming out (what is impolitely known as 'fanny farting'!) and it was never like that in the movies when they saw couples making love.

Male ostomates

The importance of sex to men was dramatically illustrated by a panel of male paraplegics. When asked if they were given the choice between getting back their ability to walk or their normal sexual functioning, all chose sex. Developing a satisfactory sex life is not always easy for people, with or without surgery. The male ostomate should be aware that factors other than the ostomy can be responsible for the problems. For example, how good is the relationship now and how was it before surgery? How was erectile functioning before surgery? How are you functioning in masturbation? Do you have morning erections? Have you checked with your surgeon as to whether there has been any severing of the nerves that facilitate erectile functioning? Sometimes it is difficult to talk to your doctor about sexual matters – so, above all, you need a doctor with whom you have a good relationship.

I recall counselling a twenty-four-year-old with quite significant erectile problems who had never had sexual intercourse. He told me he had gone to his doctor who had sent him off, having chastised him for bothering him, and had said to him: "There's more to life than sex!" Part of my advice to him was to change doctors, as there are thousands of sympathetic caring doctors out there.

If there is no physical reason for your erectile problems, the most important thing is *do not panic*. I am often struck how quickly the loss of an erection becomes a big problem for men. There is an old joke that defines panic as 'not the first time you cannot do it twice, but the second time you cannot do it once', and this is so true. I have had men come in to see me who have had one 'failure', as they called it, and were already in a panic. When I ask them what they feel if their girlfriend does not have an orgasm, it is an entirely different story, as they see *that* as quite normal.

You can build up your confidence through masturbation, relaxation, fantasy exercises and by confronting your fear by talking about it to a partner, particularly away from the bedroom. What I call 'pleasuring exercises' can also help. In these exercises, you put a ban on sexual intercourse no matter what happens and this can be very freeing from the male performance point of view. Don't panic either if you are getting an erection but then losing it again. It is not the last erection you are ever going to have. It's like the 15B bus– which covers the area where I live – it's fairly reliable and there will be another one along in a few minutes.

What if, for medical reasons, there is no possibility of erectile functioning returning? In my experience of working with men who have erectile dysfunction, listening to what they tell me, and observing the understanding they have gained of the woman's body, it seems to me that they can make far better lovers than a lot of men without problems. They tell me their partners appear to be very satisfied with the lovemaking, although naturally they would like to have the option of sexual intercourse. But there are lots and lots of ways of pleasuring a woman. Hopefully you have not lost the use of your fingers, hands, tongues or lips and an awful lot of pleasure can be given with all of these. If, up until now, you have been a bit remiss about all of this, now is a very good time to be creative and to initiate some change in your lovemaking when you are still in the process of change yourself. And do remember all the times when you were young and car windows got steamed up, usually as a result of just kissing and fondling!

Medically you have the option of Viagra, injections, prosthesis or the vacuum pump, all discussed in detail in *Chapter 4*. In a lot of cases, however, Viagra and penile injections do not work due to nerve damage from surgery and although the use of penile prosthesis by ostomates is routine in the US, it is in its infancy here. So by far the most effective device is the vacuum pump. A plastic cylinder fits over the penis, a lever is pressed that pumps air out of the cylinder creating a vacuum that draws blood into the penis, thereby creating an erection. A constricting ring is placed at the base of the penis, which keeps it erect, and the vacuum pump is then removed. Initially, this is pretty daunting to look at. However, it can be very effective in producing and maintaining an erection, particularly if you have a loving partner. Also, there are no side effects and you are not putting any chemicals into your body.

After surgery, retrograde ejaculation can occur whereby the man knows he is ejaculating but the ejaculate does not come out through the penis. Instead it goes back into the system. This should be talked over with your urologist or doctor.

I would like to conclude this chapter by quoting feminist writer Leonore Tiefer, who is a professor of urology and psychiatry at the Albert Einstein College of Medicine in the Bronx and who is also a psychologist. She says:

> "For every dollar devoted to perfecting the phallus, I would like to insist that a dollar be devoted to assisting women with their complaints about partner impairments in kissing, tenderness, talk, hygiene, and general eroticism. Too many men still can't dance, write love poems, erotically massage the clitoris, or diaper the baby and let Mom get some rest."

Professor Tiefer warns that continuing to "avoid dealing with women's sexuality and sexuality from women's point of view... perpetuates sexology as concerned only with coital performance, perpetuates the erection as a be-all and end-all of sexual relations, and continues the tradition of heavy medical investment in perfecting the penis. From the feminist point of view, it is rearranging the deck chairs on the *Titanic*".

[11]

THE AGEING
PROCESS AND
SEXUALITY

S ome time ago I was at a conference on ageing and sexuality. One of the speakers asked us how many of us had
parents still alive and if we visited them regularly. A lot
of hands shot up. She then asked us if we used our key when
calling on them or if we knocked at the door to alert them.
Practically everybody said they just used their key. "And would
it ever dawn on you that they might be having sex at the
time?" she asked. Horrified gasps. Not our parents. Not our
ageing parents!

She went on to suggest that, as night time is the time when
our bodies are at their most tired and as retired people often
take a rest in the afternoon and usually have nobody else other
than their partners living with them, it is quite within the
bounds of possibility that the couple may be having sex in the
afternoon. We became a bit more thoughtful as we recognised
the sense in what she said. Now, we were all psychosexual therapists and I use this example deliberately to show how
predisposed we all are, even specialists in the field, to thinking
that sex is primarily for the young and for the body beautiful
and how we must work at realising that it is for all ages and
continues to be enjoyed by a great variety of people – either alone
or together. Indeed, my oldest client was a seventy-eight-year-

THE AGEING PROCESS AND SEXUALITY

old man who came to see me, as he was concerned that he was masturbating rather a lot – it was once a day as I recall – and he felt that he was being unfair to his wife, as she had MS and was wheelchair bound.

Menopause

One of the first indications of approaching middle age in women is the onset of menopause and this can give rise to various problems, such as dryness and painful intercourse, which can affect the couple sexually. I know that these conditions are specific to women but, as with all sexual problems, they have an affect on the couple as well. Most of the problems can be treated by your GP, although in some cases you may require more specific treatment from a sex therapist, particularly if you have allowed the condition to continue for a period of time. Bear in mind that your hormone levels decrease with the onset of menopause, and the lowered oestrogen levels mean that there is a decrease in the blood supply to the vagina and the nerves and glands around it. This makes the delicate tissue in that area thinner and drier and less able to produce the normal secretions that help you to lubricate before and during intercourse. So, if you are having some pain in connection with intercourse this is quite normal, but it can be avoided either by using a lubricant, an oestrogen cream or some form of hormonal replacement therapy. Your GP will be the one to advise you, but remember *you* must bring up the subject with him or her. Having known you for a number of years, your GP is not suddenly going to start showing an interest in your sex life. And no, they will not be embarrassed by your bringing up the subject. They are human beings too with their own sex lives. The alternative medicine route is also available and some women are much happier getting their hormone replacement in health food stores or from an alternative medicine practitioner.

For some women, but by no means all, menopause brings a decrease in sexual activity. As a general rule, if a woman has enjoyed a fairly healthy sexual life before menopause it is most likely that she will continue to do so after the menopause. The trouble is that some people have short memories and see the menopause as a convenient excuse to justify a problem that was there all along. It is important to differentiate between lack of desire and loss of sex drive. Men and women can still experience sex drive without desire – they can be aware of sexual feelings and thoughts, but not in connection with their partner. I would hold that it is quite normal not to feel desire for your partner all the time, particularly if you have been lovers for years. It is somewhat unrealistic to expect sex to be always passionate and full of thrills when you both know each other inside out. Loss of desire can occur for many reasons – illness, pain and discomfort, depression or simply the attitudes that I wrote of at the beginning of this chapter, which can make an elderly couple believe that they should be really past it by now. And if the couple's lovemaking has become routine and boring, it is quite natural to be fed up with it. Imagine eating the same things for dinner day after day! No matter how much you like it, you will eventually grow tired of it. So seek a little variety. It may be just changing the time of day when you make love, it may be using a different room, it may be having sex with the lights off instead of on, or on instead of off. Occasionally take it in turns to come up with a new suggestion and see where that takes you.

Body image

Body image is something that can cause problems with ageing, particularly in women, and especially if she has put on weight, which woman tend to do as they age. This was brought home to me recently when Ian was referred to me suffering with erectile problems. He was severely overweight, but told me that he had always been like that. He told me that he and his wife, Vera, had always been madly in love, almost to the exclusion of everybody else, including their daughter and son. Some time previously, he had been sent overseas on a work assignment and there was an awful lot of sex on offer. He felt that, sexually, he had to shut himself down totally as he did not want to be unfaithful to his wife – this shutting down even included masturbation. When he came home for an occasional weekend, he found he was also avoiding being sexual, but did not realise he had a problem until he came home at the end of the assignment and could not get an erection. Given the intensity of his feelings for his wife this all made sense to me, dramatic as it was. However, when I saw Vera, who was a very attractive woman, she told me that she knew the problem was to do with *her* and she knew his erectile difficulties stemmed from his seeing her nude body now that she had put on some weight. When he had married her she had been a very slim and very attractive young woman with a twenty-inch waist. Now that she was menopausal how could he possibly fancy her? And so on. In point of fact, she was not very much overweight but had convinced herself of her unattractiveness.

Another area where body image may cause a problem is if the older person has entered into a new relationship with a much younger person. This can be a particular problem if the woman is the older partner, as she may feel somewhat inhibited in revealing all, when 'all' could include stretch marks, hysterectomy scars, cellulite and anything else that detracts from the body-beautiful image.

However, the new partner does not necessarily have to be younger – new relationships in later life can cause all sorts of problems. Both people are bringing their own history to the new relationship. They will either be widowed, separated or coming from a previous long-term relationship and, if they have not, then they will have spent a long time living alone and may have become quite set in how and when they do things. Both will also have a sexual history and this can cause problems between the new couple. For instance, the man will sometimes feel guilty about being sexual with somebody new, even though, at the same time, he very much wants to make love with his new partner, and erectile problems can ensue. I remember one client who was madly in love with his new partner, having been widowed a few years previously from a wife he also loved very much. He still felt desperately sad about his wife's death and guilty at the extent of her suffering. He could not get an erection at all and it took a number of sessions in therapy before he was able to learn to relax enough to let go of the past and allow himself the pleasure of being fully sexual again. He really needed the understanding of his girlfriend through all of this.

There can also be a lot of anxiety generated by one or other feeling that they are not as good sexually as the previous partner and it takes a lot of reassurance in order for this idea not to take on a life of its own. Often too, one or other, or both, may not have been sexual for a long time and can be very apprehensive about their performance, and fear of rejection can be very high. I remember one client being terribly anxious about her new relationship, which was about to become sexual. She had married very young and her husband had been her only sexual partner. Now she was faced with using condoms for the first time, having sex again after a long gap and was worried about what the new man in her life would say about her body which had given birth to three children and was a bit out of shape. To add to her worries, her children still lived at home and they were finding it difficult to accept this new man in her life.

Medical conditions

For either partner, medical conditions are another hazard in the ageing process. Cardiovascular disease, cancer, diabetes and arthritis are just some of the conditions that become more likely as we get older and it is particularly scary when the conditions that were afflicting one's parents are now part of one's own story.

The immediate concern whenever an illness strikes is dealing with the illness but, when that has been taken care of and the reins of ordinary living are taken up again, it is important that the sex life of the couple is not forgotten. Of course, it is often in an altered state and adjustments need to be made. For example, if either of you have had hip surgery, different positions will have to be investigated. Look on it as a challenge. The 'spoons' position where the woman lies with her back to the man and his penis enters her vagina from behind can be very enjoyable in this instance. Or if you are feeling a little more adventurous, try the T-position (see *Figure 12* below). In this position the man lies on his side and the woman on her back, but lying across him (forming a T) with her legs over his body. She does the moving and so it is also good if he has a back problem. Another excellent position is when the couple lie side by side, but facing each other, and the woman puts her leg over his. It is a very comfortable position that does not require a lot of energy and yet can produce very intense sensations.

Figure 12
T-position.

A little about the ageing penis. As it enters mid-life some changes occur. It may need more stimulation than before in order to get hard. It may not get as firm as it used to and it may be easier for it to lose its hardness. The angle of erection may not be as elevated. The need for orgasm is less intense and the force of ejaculation and amount of ejaculate is reduced. These changes occur very gradually over a couple of decades and all are normal. After all, your body is getting older too; you may be losing your hair, your teeth need more attention, perhaps you are wearing glasses. So don't get into a tizzy about it and don't expect too much from your poor penis. It is not the penis you had at twenty, but then neither is any other part of you! However, as a man, you are still capable of giving and receiving as much erotic pleasure as you ever were and that is much more important than anything else in the scheme of things. In fact, some women would say that older men make better lovers as they are more considerate, more patient and, of course, more mature mentally than the younger studs who are more concerned with their own enjoyment than that of the woman's. They also have usually reached where they want to be in their lives and are less likely to be tied up with proving themselves.

It is important to remember that research has consistently shown that regular sexual activity (sex or masturbation once or twice a week) seems to keep the vagina moist, elastic and more easily lubricated. Therefore, any kind of sexual arousal, whether it is from reading, fantasy or watching an erotic film, will increase the blood flow to the genital area and help maintain genital and penile health. For a lot of couples, middle age and the menopause bring an end to childbearing years and the possibility, perhaps for the first time, of being sexual without the fear of pregnancy. Children have often left home leaving the couple more time for themselves, and with people retiring earlier and earlier, people have more leisure time, more time for holidays and, therefore, more time to be sexual without the tiredness that often used to accompany it. So it helps to look at the menopause and ageing, not as a roadblock to sexuality, but merely as a detour on a lifelong journey.

As Robert Browning's Rabbi Ben Ezra puts it:

> "Grow old along with me, the best is yet to be
> The last of life for which the first was made."

ABUSE AND ITS AFFECT ON SEXUALITY

If you, or your partner, have been abused and you are experiencing sexual difficulties, you can be pretty sure that the abuse is a contributory factor. Here are the case histories of some people I have worked with.

■ **Mary** was a twenty-six year old secretary who came to see me because she was having a problem whenever it got to the sexual intercourse stage with a boyfriend. She seemed to encourage them until it got to the point of becoming really intimate and then she would cut off all contact. She would then start the process all over again with somebody else – the chase, the catch, getting him aroused and close to intercourse, and then suddenly pulling back. She was quickly earning a reputation as a tease in her hometown and did not want to be this way. Mary apparently had a lovely body. I say 'apparently' because she dressed in such a way that no shape was visible. Her blouse was always buttoned up to the top and she always wore trousers. She had one 'interview skirt' in her wardrobe and all her blouses were similar – she just had one for every day of the week. When I enquired about her underwear I found out that it was purely functional. Her hair was cut as short as her hairdresser could manage and she wore no make up. In other words there was no hint of her femininity. Although she was potentially very attractive, Mary found it very difficult to talk to me or to meet my eye and it took months of work with her before she was able to tell me her story. This involved abuse by her brother and, subsequently, by her cousin, which her brother had arranged. She still lived at home on the family farm and that particular brother had built a house on the land, where he lived with his wife and children. So Mary saw him all the time and each time she saw him she was reminded of the abuse. With the arrival of his daughter she began to have fears for the little one and this caused her to seek help.

■ **Eddy's** girlfriend had been a client of mine and, some time after I finished working with her, he made an appointment to see me. He was feeling very unhappy and quarrelling a lot with her and needed help to talk this through. Gradually, over a period of time, we explored his background until he felt safe enough to tell me things he had never shared with anybody before. His abuse had started when he was totally sexually inexperienced, in his early teens. He was abused by an older male colleague and this started a cycle of homosexual activity that continued into the present. As he started to tell me his story, he would frequently have to take a break as the telling was quite horrific for him involving as it did testicular mutilation, sadism, multiple rapes and other forms of degradation. He subsequently told me that he kept watching my face and if, at any moment, I had looked shocked he was prepared to stop talking. Eddy is currently coming to terms with his bisexuality.

■ **Brian** and his wife were very anxious to start a family. However, he was never able to ejaculate, no matter how long he spent on a lovemaking session. His wife was very understanding but was getting tired, in every sense of the word, of their marathon sessions. Neither had ever had sex with anybody else and so were very unsure of what they should actually be doing.

Brian's abuse had occurred when he was an altar boy. He had been fondled and made to rub his abuser's penis and, while he did not actually witness any ejaculation, he became terrified that he himself might ejaculate and this fear carried on into his later life.

■ When **Denise** came to see me she had been in intensive psychotherapy for four years as a result of childhood abuse. She had no memory at all of this abuse until one day her little niece who was visiting her was sitting on the toilet, chatting away as kids do. Denise saw the child's panties on the floor and suddenly she was back as a child herself. She had been abused in a very violent way with objects inserted in her vagina with the resultant fear that all of that brought into her young life. Her abuser was a neighbour who told her that this was what God had told him to do. When she came to see me she was happily at the end of her abuse work with her therapist, but had lost all sexual desire. She was very upset about this, and her husband, whom I also saw, felt quite apart from her.

I use these case histories to illustrate the many and varied ways that child abuse can affect people in their subsequent lives, and particularly in their sex lives. Here, in Ireland, the figures for abuse appear very high – at about one in seven. If you have been abused, and you feel it is causing you problems in your life, then I would really urge you to seek help. Making the decision to get help is the first step and one of the most difficult ones. It usually comes about because something happens in the abused person's life that makes it intolerable for them to continue to do nothing, as seen in the cases above. If you have been abused, you will probably find that you have always intended to do something about it and discuss it with someone, but you have put it off. After all, no one looks forward to abuse work, but when you reach a crisis point it becomes inevitable.

Below are some of the stages you will go through during counselling.

Breaking the silence

When you have found a suitable counsellor, one you can relate to and trust, the process of breaking the silence begins, the process of remembering and telling your story. This may be easy for you and it may all come out straightaway, or it may be incredibly difficult as you struggle with the words. The counsellor will work at whatever pace you want – sometimes just one little memory is all we can cope with at a time – and you will never be rushed. As you tell your story, you are, at the same time, beginning to acknowledge that this abuse actually happened, as this fact is often locked away because you don't wish to look at it. You must understand that the victims of abuse very often feel guilty.

I remember working with Ciara on her childhood abuse by her father, her uncle and her brother, she got very upset remembering that she was an incredibly pretty little girl with long, blonde hair. "I'm sure I used to use my looks to make them like me," she cried and she had a difficult time getting her head around the concept that, even if she did, it did not excuse what they had done to her. So the biggest, single thing to bear in mind is that *it was never your fault*. The abuser is always the older one, in a position of trust, and the abused the younger innocent person.

The trouble is that when one looks back at childhood abuse it is with the eyes of an adult, rather than the eyes of a child, and that is why all the boundaries get blurred. What I mean by that is that the adult will tend to say, "Oh my God, I remember actually physically enjoying some of the abuse, I must be depraved", but in fact what you should be saying is, "I, as a child, enjoyed it because my body physically responded to touch, but now, as an adult, I know the abuser should not have done what he did."

Childhood experimentation

Sometimes clients get quite agitated when they start to tell me about something that happened in their youth and feel that, in fact, *they* were the abuser of a sibling or a friend. I think it is very important here to make a distinction between sexual experimentation and sexual abuse. Experimentation will often take place when children are young and are trying to discover what all this body thing is about; whether their siblings are made the same as themselves, and, if they are not, what the actual difference is. This often leads to mutual touching and pleasuring; but if there is not much of a discrepancy in ages and it was all fairly innocent (although probably each of the children concerned felt that they shouldn't really be doing this) then I think it should be seen for what it was – pure experimentation.

Anger

In the course of your abuse work, you will go through a lot of emotions including anger and grief. Of course you will be angry at what was done to you, that is to be expected, but what partners of abused people find hard to understand is the fact that quite often the abused still likes the abuser and, in some cases, still even loves them.

Lost childhood

You will also experience a lot of grief because you were deprived of quite a sizeable chunk of your childhood. This will lead on to what is called 'inner child' work and, even though it sounds strange, it is a very necessary part of the process. In the course of this work, you will be encouraged to get in touch with your inner child, that is the child you once were. The counsellor will be helping you to give back to that child the emotions and feelings it never had because, through abuse, he or she was plunged into the adult world way ahead of time. I find that people often start repairing the damage to their inner child naturally by building up a close relationship with a niece or a nephew and through this relationship they are enabled to re-live their own childhood to a certain extent.

I remember Pat who had suffered great physical and verbal abuse at the hands of his father and was really damaged by it. Pat had a nephew he really adored. He took this child swimming, brought him to football matches and did with him all the things that Pat's dad had not done with him when he was a child. He found it very easy to do this and explained to me that it was fine to buy himself a little piece of Lego or a toy car at the same time as buying his nephew one, and then they both played with them! He was already doing all of this when we started to discuss what he might do to nurture the child within himself and was really pleased with his own instincts.

I particularly remember Sheila who had just come out of an abusive marriage and had previously been abused by her two brothers. She took great delight in using her shopping trolley as a skating vehicle and careered up and down the aisles, much to the dismay of her four children!

Discovering or rediscovering play as Pat and Sheila did is, of course, the lighter side of the abuse work, but it is nonetheless an important part of it.

Confrontation

Confronting the abuser is an area that is fraught with danger. There comes a time when, after a lot of the remembering, believing, anger and grieving work has been done, the question of confrontation comes up. Sometimes the abuser is already deceased and the question does not arise, but, in many cases, they are often still alive and the abused person may feel the need to confront them in order to move on with their own lives. The problem is that the abused has to be prepared for various types of response from the abuser, and one of these is total denial. Another response may be to give a totally different version of events from those that actually happened. So different outcomes have to be envisaged and acted out in the counselling room before any actual confrontation takes place, to ensure that the abused feels able to cope. I would see face-to-face confrontation of the abuser as a last resort, a step which cannot be taken lightly and which should be rehearsed very well beforehand if it has to take place.

Forgiveness

During therapy the question of forgiveness, of course, arises. Some people feel the need to forgive, while for others it is simply out of the question. Suffice to say that it is not a necessary part of the work, more an optional extra. Whatever the particular person feels most comfortable with is what is right for them, for what they want to achieve is to be able to get on with their lives without the awful sense of being a victim hanging over them. And that is what comes about after all the work – moving on. The memory that you have suffered abuse may never go away completely but, hopefully, the load will be made bearable. So do seek help if you are one of those people who have suffered abuse.

Partners

Let us not forget the partners of the abused. Sometimes these partners attend counselling with the abused person throughout the abuse work but, more often, they do not. Indeed sometimes, the abused wants to keep the identity of the abuser a secret from the partner as they feel it will interfere too much with intricate family or business relationships. So if the partner is not attending counselling (and some of the larger centres like the Rape Crisis offer support groups for partners of abused people) they can feel quite isolated and helpless. They see their loved one coming home from counselling, emotional but not wanting to talk about it, and they wonder what they can do. If you are the partner of an abused person, never underestimate the power of just *being* there, particularly if you are a male partner of an abused female. Men like to offer solutions and like to do something, so just being there is a difficult concept for them but, believe me, it is really the very best thing you can do. If you are the abused, try to be aware that your partner has very little idea of what you are going through but wants to help at the same time. As our tutors used to say to my group when we were training as counsellors and were heading home after a very intensive period of training, "Be kind to those you are going home to – remember they haven't been here."

In this section I have discussed some of the emotions that you will go through when you decide to seek help for the abuse you suffered as a child. Ask for help. You will be really glad that you did.

[13]

SEXUAL
POSITIONS

Variety is the spice of life and nowhere is this more appropriate than in lovemaking. If you take any monogamous relationship lasting, say, forty-five years and estimate that the couple make love on average twice a week, then in a lifetime together they will have made love over four thousand times. If the couple do this more or less the same way each time, it is fairly obvious that they will become bored and less inclined to do it. Having said that, everybody has their favourite positions to which they return again and again, either because they give them particular pleasure or they know that it helps them to reach a climax or because they are just plain comfortable.

Some sex manuals would have us believe that there are hundreds of different positions, which can be quite intimidating, but if you look closely at the instructions you will find that lots of the positions they outline are just variations on the previous position. There are many reasons for using different positions: to alter the angle of the penis in the vagina causing a variety of sensations, to provide more accessibility to various body parts like breasts and buttocks, to help with things like bad backs or physical disabilities, and so on – so do experiment.

Let us divide the positions into six sections.

Woman on top

Nancy Friday's excellent book on female fantasies is called
Women On Top (Hutchinson, London, 1991), which I think is
very indicative of where we have moved to sexually. It is now
one of women's favourite positions and gets away from the
whole idea of the woman just lying there and putting up with
sex just to please her man. From the man's point of view, this is
a great position as he can lie there and be made love to, which
is very appealing! The woman is very often much lighter than
her man so it is great for her not to have to take all his weight.

Below are some ideas for positions with the woman on top.

Figure 13
The woman makes
love to the man
with her legs on
either side of him
sitting upright. In
this position, not
only does he have
a great view of her
breasts, but is free
to play with them.

Figure 14
The woman bends
over the man, which
allows her to kiss
him and to rub
her breasts over
his body.

167

Figure 15
The woman sits
with her legs
over the man's
shoulders.

Figure 16
The woman
sits astride the
man but facing
away from him.

Figure 17
The woman lies
flat on top of the
man with their
pubic bones
touching. His legs
are closed and
hers are down
each side of his.

Man on top

This is what is called 'the missionary position'. The story goes
that, when the missionaries first went to third world countries,
the natives spied on them and found it amusing that they used
only this position. The 'uncivilised' people were far less inhibited
and were used to lots of variety in their sexual acts. It is, of
course, a very popular position enabling the man to take the
lead and be masterful. The most basic way of achieving this
position is for the woman to lie flat with her legs apart and the
man to lie inside her.

Figure 18
Missionary position
with the woman's
legs drawn up.

Figure 19
Variation of
missionary
position.

Figure 20
The woman puts her legs up over the man's hips or waist, which allows for deeper penetration.

Figure 21
The woman puts her legs up over the man's shoulders, which allows for even deeper penetration.

Figure 22
The man kneels on the floor and the woman sits on the side of the bed with her legs around his waist.

With any of these positions a pillow placed underneath the woman's bottom will help her to feel more stimulated as the thrusting will be at a different angle and she will feel more strongly the indirect stimulation of her clitoris. If, at any stage, in the man-on-top position the woman closes her legs more tightly, her partner's penis will get additional stimulation.

Rear Entry

This is not to be confused with anal sex but is rather the penis entering the vagina with the man behind the woman. Some women are very put off by this as they find it rather animalistic but for some it is very exciting and many men find the rear view of their partner particularly arousing. For this position, the woman kneels on the bed and leans forward with her head on a pillow. The man kneels behind her and slowly enters her. In this position he can stimulate her breasts, clitoris and her buttocks, as in *Figure 23*.

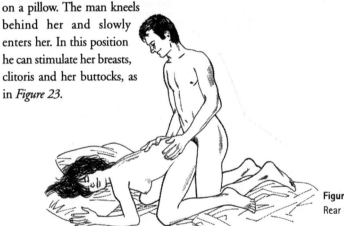

Figure 23
Rear entry.

A variation is for her to rest the upper part of her body on the bed or sofa and kneel on the floor, using a cushion or pillow to ensure her knees are comfortable. She is not able to move her body much in this position, but she can use her hips to thrust quite vigorously.

171

Side by side

Couples find side-by-side positions very intimate. They can cause a lot of hilarity, as the penis often pops out and needs to be put in again. In side-by-side positions, the couple are facing each other, so kissing is very much on the cards, which adds to the intimacy. It is also a useful position when the woman is pregnant and the tummy starts to get in the way. One of these positons is the T-position, where the woman lies on her back, or turned a little towards her partner, and he lies on his side with his legs under her bottom, which allows her to put her legs over his (see *Figure 12* on *page 155*). Another side-by-side position is shown in *Figure 9* on *page 104*.

Figure 24
Another side-by-side position is for both partners to be on their sides but he enters her half from behind and half from the side, with one of his legs through hers.

Standing

There is no truth in the statement that it is not possible to get pregnant if you do it standing up! However, there is a sense of the forbidden about this position, which makes it more exciting. Clients have told me of great quickies they have had – particularly in offices for some reason – when they were standing up. If only filing cabinets could talk, they would probably have quite a story to tell in some business houses! If you are making love standing up, then the woman will probably need to lean against something and if there is a great discrepancy in the couple's height then a new use can be found for the telephone book.

Rear entry standing up is also an option, particularly if she bends over and leans on something like a table for support.

Figure 25
This is a very erotic position. The man picks up the woman, his arms around her waist and she puts her arms around his neck and her legs around his body. Obviously only for the very fit and supple of body.

And Finally!

No section on positions would be complete without reference to the famous '69'. This is where the couple give oral sex to each other simultaneously. As a male client said to me, "Love doing it, not much of a view."

Figure 26
'69'.

These are a few ways to add variety to your sex life, so do experiment.

[14]

SEX SHOULD
BE FUN

One of my main aims when working with people is to help them discover or, in some cases, rediscover that sex can and should be fun. I often think that, if I had to describe how we are sexual together to a person from another planet, they would be incredulous. "You do *what* to each other?" It all sounds a bit crazy. But it *is* fun, it's free, you don't need a babysitter if you have children, it is great for burning calories and it makes a couple feel much closer. However, people get very uptight about their performances and feel they are 'no good at it'. There is no such thing as 'no good at it' in my opinion – it is just what is good for the person or the couple. As a friend of mine puts it, "Making love is like making brown bread – sometimes it turns out better than others but its always good for you."

To continue the food analogy, we should bring variety to our sex lives just as we bring variety to our diets. If you are in a long-term relationship, making love to the same person over a long period of time can become boring, so just as we vary the food we eat, we should also add variety to our sex lives. For instance, no matter how much you love Thai food you will not want to eat it every night and no matter how much you love somebody, you will not be happy doing the same thing with them every night. So what can you do to spice up your sex lives, and therefore add to the enjoyment and fun of the experience? Some of the things I will suggest may not be right for you, and you don't have to try them all, but consider them and take your pick. Or give your partner their choice – you will probably be surprised at their selection!

Change of venue

Despite our inventiveness with locations early on in our lives, particularly when there is no place readily available, our relationships develop we tend to settle into a rather dull routine. Couples usually tell me they make love in the bedroom, either late at night or early in the morning, with clothes off and the light on. So how about initiating a few changes? Do you have a spare room? Have you ever made love in it? This is quite different from using the spare room because there has been a row or the partner is snoring or you came in very late and don't want to disturb him or her (or be found out as to how late it actually was when you got in!). How about having a bath or a shower together? And remember that some great sessions can be held in front of the fire, but be sure you are not likely to be disturbed. I remember one of my clients telling me that she had decided that when her husband came home from the rugby match she would be already showered and in her dressing gown and ready for their 'homework'. She lit the fire, spread a duvet on the floor and surrounded it with candles. She felt it would be really nice there and they would get their session done before they went out for the evening. Imagine her horror when he arrived in with a gang of the lads, who had been at the match, for a quick beer. The lads were very impressed and only sorry that they were not going home to the same treatment. They were not to know that the couple had serious sex problems and the guy's image went right up among his friends.

175

Have you ever thought of sex outdoors? That, too, could be scary but can add a certain excitement to the proceedings. Or, if funds allow, book into a hotel or guesthouse for no specific reason and maybe play a game pretending that you have only just met, or that you are with another partner and this is an illicit meeting. Role-playing can be fun. For variety, one couple I know sometimes go to a bar and pretend to be brother and sister. They see if they can still attract the opposite sex, but have the excuse that they have to leave together.

Fantasy

Talk of role-playing leads on naturally enough to fantasy. This is a word that gives people a lot of anxiety. For instance people can be concerned that, if they fantasise about somebody, they are in some way being unfaithful to their partner. I do not agree with this viewpoint. After all, nobody is being hurt and it can lead to higher levels of arousal and, therefore, better sex. Of course, it would be harmful if it were to cease being a fantasy and became a reality and, instead of just fantasising of being with somebody else, you went and had sex with that person.

People say to me that they have no imagination and, therefore, cannot fantasise. However, when I ask them how they would spend their winnings if they won the lottery, they have absolutely no difficulty. So what they are really talking about is having no sexual fantasy. Sometimes I suggest that they use some reading material to assist them in their fantasies. This can be anything from that erotic scene in *Lady Chatterley's Lover*, where they make love for the second time; to some very gentle romantic story; or actual sexual fantasies, such as any of the Nancy Friday books or some of the Black Lace books. Videos can also be used as an aid to sexual fantasy. A couple could watch a movie that has good sexual content together, then take over themselves and play out the roles. Remember you are writing your own script and there is no right or wrong, only fun. And how about a couple developing their own fantasy? For example, the woman might begin by saying, "I'm staying overnight to attend a conference and I go to my room for an early night." He may then wish to carry on with, "I knock at your door to ask if I can use your phone – mine is not working and I want to order room service." Take it from there and goodness knows where it may lead!

Another type of fantasy might involve dressing up and playing out a role with one or both of the partners dressing up. As some people might not be comfortable with this, a version of it could be to use underwear, which is kept on while making love, or slowly removed. And it doesn't have to be underwear that makes the woman feel like some sex object from a porn movie. There are loads of beautiful underwear sets available in your local store – anything that makes you feel good will certainly help your mate to feel good, too. But at least have it matching. When I go to the gym, I am constantly saddened to see these bodies, which the women are working so hard at getting in shape, being clothed in grey, dreary underwear. Even if nobody is ever going to see your underwear, you owe it to yourself to be pleased when you look in the mirror. Hold up stockings are another option and certainly make a woman feel sexier than tights. These, together with high-heeled shoes, might be left on while making love.

Be inventive!

Sex, of course, does not have to include intercourse. In fact, intercourse is really only necessary if a couple are trying to have a baby – and that is not strictly true any more in these fertility-assisted days. So try agreeing beforehand that there will be no intercourse, and that the emphasis will be on giving and receiving pleasure in all other ways. A variation on this would be to decide that you will only give and receive a massage. This has to be preceded by a bath or a shower (try taking it together if there is room, or even if there isn't) and make sure you have nice soft lighting, a warmer than usual room, music playing and proceed to give each other a full body massage, front and back, with the only talk being about what you like or don't like. Use body lotions or oils but be sure to warm them first by taking them into the bath or shower with you – it's a big turn-off to suddenly get a very cold lotion on your body. No matter how much you want to proceed on to being sexual, do not. It will make the next time you do (probably the next morning) so much better. While working with a visually impaired woman recently, I was struck by how sensitive she was to touch. Bearing this in mind, it could be really rewarding to give or receive a massage while blindfolded. Improvise with a scarf if you have no blindfold.

Quickies

Be open to the suggestion of a quickie. As you know sometimes we want a three-course meal or even a banquet, but sometimes we really only want a sandwich! The same applies to sex. This encounter could definitely take place in a venue that you would not normally choose; a lot of the clothes are left on and there can really be a sense of being bold. Cast your mind back to all those times when you thought your parents were going to come in and catch you in the middle of sexual activity and you get the message.

Emily told me about a previous married lover that she had, and how he liked to be spontaneous. She got a call one day at eight in the morning having just stepped out of the shower. She had an important meeting scheduled for nine-thirty. Her lover told her he was in the car outside and really wanted to see her. As he was the one who usually had deadlines, she found it very exhilarating to make love on the sofa – they didn't have time to go upstairs – and then attend her meeting knowing what she had been doing forty-five minutes prior to that. Another client told me that going home during his lunch break for a quickie gave a whole new meaning to a lunch roll!

Telephone sex

The book *Vox* by Nicholson Baker consists entirely of a telephone conversation between two strangers who have phone sex and was, I suppose, a precursor to sex on the internet. However, sex on the telephone between two people who are already lovers can be equally erotic. Some people use it when they are apart to tell each other what they would like to be doing if they were together, but it can work equally well if they are using the telephone to suggest what they might be doing later. If you saw the film *The Truth About Cats and Dogs* (1996), you will remember a great scene where the couple are masturbating while having telephone sex. It is very beautifully done and might give you some more ideas. If you are a bit shy about being specific face-to-face, then the telephone might be a great help, suggestive text messages can also be fun. And think what a turn-on it will be for your partner if, sexually, you are usually the reticent one.

I remember a client telling me about a previous boyfriend. He telephoned her one day and asked her to come around that evening at eleven o'clock. He would leave the front door slightly open and would be waiting for her inside, but she was to say absolutely nothing. She did as requested and they made very passionate love on the couch in his living room, without saying anything at all, and then she left. The fact that his eleven-year-old son was visiting him and was asleep in another room made it all the more exciting!

Visit a sex shop

When you were young, a visit to a toyshop was always exciting. So, now that you are grown up, why not visit a sex toyshop? I hope that the view that they are somewhat seedy places full of nasty men in raincoats has receded by now – although, unfortunately, not completely, from what people say to me. It can be great fun to go there, either with a partner or with a friend because it's easier to laugh when you are with somebody else. There are all sorts of toys and sex aids on show, some fun, some ridiculous, but all worth considering. (I remember the first time I went to one with a male friend and being amazed at the number of male vibrators that were available. I had thought this was a purely female domain. "Our hands get tired too you know," said my friend.) Probably the biggest seller in most sex shops is the vibrator and this, too, can add variety to your sex life. It should not be used all the time but it can make things a bit different. Either the male can use it on the female or he can watch her use it herself – again that is not something everybody is comfortable with, but it may work for you. There are also available some very good body massagers which double up as vibrators and they can be used in conjunction with a massage.

Also available from the sex shop are different types of edible toys, but real food can also add something different to your sex life, depending on your taste. Chocolate is a great favourite, spread on and licked off; interesting things can be done with strawberries, ice cubes, champagne… the list is endless. All it needs is a little imagination and a sense of adventure. And for the less adventurous, sometimes even a simple cup of tea and slice of toast brought to the partner in bed when not expected can lead to a most rewarding conclusion!

FURTHER READING

Comfort, Alex *The Joy of Sex* (London: Quartet Books Ltd) 1996.

Dalvin, Dr David *The Book of Love* (Great Britain: New English Library Ltd.) 1974.

Friday, Nancy *My Secret Garden* (London: Hutchinson/Random House) 1979.

– *Men in Love: Their Secret Fantasies* (London: Hutchinson/Random House) 1980.

– *Women on Top* (London: Hutchinson/Random House) 1991.

Ileostomy and Internal Pouch Support Group (ia)
Going Home: Living with an Ileostomy (Scunthorpe, England: Ileostomy and Internal Pouch Support Group) 1996.

Zilbergeld, Bernie *The New Male Sexuality* – revised edition (New York: Bantam/Random House) 1999.

INDEX

A

B

C

K
Kegels exercise, 65, 67, 73, 87, 88, 90, 91, 96
kissing, 39, 148, 149, 172

L
libido, 13, 16, 48, 121, 123, 152

M
masturbation, 17, 156
  men, 22, 32, 46, 62, 74, 147
  women, 20–21, 39, 101, 104, 112, 145
menopause, 151–152, 156
hormone replacement therapy (HRT), 151
Mirena, 131
morning-after pill, 129–130

O
oral sex, 15, 120, 145, 173
  cunnilingus, 39–40
  fellatio, 32–33
orgasm, 11, 14–15, 39, 42, , 81, 111
  difficulties, 14–15, 101–114
  exercises, 106–111
  faking, 25, 106
  multiple, 42, 102
  simultaneous, 16
ostomates, 139–140
  females, 144–146
  Ileostomy & Internal Pouch Support Group
    Going Home: Living with an Ileostomy, 144
  males, 146–149
outdoor sex, 176

P
painful intercourse, 124, 145, 151

S

Semans, Dr James, 65
sensate focus, 57, 62, 94, 115, 118
sex shops, 180
sexual abuse, 18–19, 83, 158–165
      case histories, 158–160
      counselling, 161–165
sex aids/toys, see fantasy, sex shops
      food, 180
      vibrator, 20, 39, 63, 103, 111–112, 114, 180
sexual dysfunction, see erectile dysfunction, vaginismus
sexually transmitted disease, 125
sexual myths, 13–24
sexual positions, 29–30, 39, 103, 112–114, 122, 146, 155, 166–173
sterilisation, 132
stress, 14, 45, 47–48, 117, 135, 140

T

telephone sex, 180
test-tube babies, 134–138
tiredness, 14, 45, 47–48, 117, 135, 140
Tiefer, Professor Leonore, 148–149
transsexual, 23–24
transvestite, 23
tubal ligation, 133

U

underwear
      women's underwear, 42, 158, 177
      men who wear women's underwear, 22–24
uprima, 51

V

vacuum devices/pumps, 52, 148

vagina
>anatomy, 35–36
>clitoris, 38–39, 41
>G-Spot, 40–42
>lubrication, 25, 38, 146, 151

vaginismus, 16, 19, 49, 76–100, 124, 142
>exercises, 83–99
>treatment of, 81–83
>vaginal trainers, 90–91

vasectomy, 133
Viagra, 44, 46, 50–51, 148
Vibrator, 20, 39, 63, 103, 111–112, 114, 180

Y
Yohimbine, 51

Z
Zilbergeld, Bernie
>*The New Male Sexuality*, 92